Measure, For Measure

Measure, For Measure

William Shakespeare

MEASURE, FOR MEASURE

Published in the United States by IndyPublish.com
Boston, Massachusetts

Published in May 2008

ISBN 1-4378-2569-9 (hardcover)

ACTUS PRIMUS

Scena prima.

Enter Duke, Escalus, Lords.

Duke. Escalus

Esc. My Lord

Duk. Of Gouernment, the properties to vnfold,
    Would seeme in me t' affect speech & discourse,
    Since I am put to know, that your owne Science
    Exceedes (in that) the lists of all aduice
    My strength can giue you: Then no more remaines
    But that, to your sufficiency, as your worth is able,
    And let them worke: The nature of our People,
    Our Cities Institutions, and the Termes
    For Common Iustice, y'are as pregnant in
    As Art, and practise, hath inriched any
    That we remember: There is our Commission,
    From which, we would not haue you warpe; call hither,

    I say, bid come before vs Angelo:
    What figure of vs thinke you, he will beare.
    For you must know, we haue with speciall soule
    Elected him our absence to supply;
    Lent him our terror, drest him with our loue,
    And giuen his Deputation all the Organs
    Of our owne powre: What thinke you of it?
Esc. If any in Vienna be of worth
  To vndergoe such ample grace, and honour,
  It is Lord Angelo.

Enter Angelo.

Duk. Looke where he comes

Ang. Always obedient to your Graces will,
  I come to know your pleasure

Duke. Angelo:
  There is a kinde of Character in thy life,
  That to th' obseruer, doth thy history
  Fully vnfold: Thy selfe, and thy belongings
  Are not thine owne so proper, as to waste
  Thy selfe vpon thy vertues; they on thee:
  Heauen doth with vs, as we, with Torches doe,
  Not light them for themselues: For if our vertues
  Did not goe forth of vs, 'twere all alike
  As if we had them not: Spirits are not finely touch'd,
  But to fine issues: nor nature neuer lends
  The smallest scruple of her excellence,
  But like a thrifty goddesse, she determines
  Her selfe the glory of a creditour,
  Both thanks, and vse; but I do bend my speech
  To one that can my part in him aduertise;
  Hold therefore Angelo:
  In our remoue, be thou at full, our selfe:
  Mortallitie and Mercie in Vienna

Liue in thy tongue, and heart: Old Escalus
Though first in question, is thy secondary.
Take thy Commission

Ang. Now good my Lord
Let there be some more test, made of my mettle,
Before so noble, and so great a figure
Be stamp't vpon it

Duk. No more euasion:
We haue with a leauen'd, and prepared choice
Proceeded to you; therefore take your honors:
Our haste from hence is of so quicke condition,
That it prefers it selfe, and leaues vnquestion'd
Matters of needfull value: We shall write to you
As time, and our concernings shall importune,
How it goes with vs, and doe looke to know
What doth befall you here. So fare you well:
To th' hopefull execution doe I leaue you,
Of your Commissions

Ang. Yet giue leaue (my Lord,)
That we may bring you something on the way

Duk. My haste may not admit it,
Nor neede you (on mine honor) haue to doe
With any scruple: your scope is as mine owne,
So to inforce, or qualifie the Lawes
As to your soule seemes good: Giue me your hand,
Ile priuily away: I loue the people,
But doe not like to stage me to their eyes:
Though it doe well, I doe not rellish well
Their lowd applause, and Aues vehement:
Nor doe I thinke the man of safe discretion
That do's affect it. Once more fare you well

Ang. The heauens giue safety to your purposes

Esc. Lead forth, and bring you backe in happinesse.

Enter.

Duk. I thanke you, fare you well

Esc. I shall desire you, Sir, to giue me leaue
   To haue free speech with you; and it concernes me
   To looke into the bottome of my place:
   A powre I haue, but of what strength and nature,
   I am not yet instructed

Ang. 'Tis so with me: Let vs withdraw together,
   And we may soone our satisfaction haue
   Touching that point

Esc. Ile wait vpon your honor.

Exeunt.

Scena Secunda.

Enter Lucio, and two other Gentlemen.

Luc. If the Duke, with the other Dukes, come not to composition with the
   King of Hungary, why then all them Dukes fall vpon the King

1.Gent. Heauen grant vs its peace, but not the King of Hungaries

2.Gent. Amen

Luc. Thou conclud'st like the Sanctimonious Pirat, that went to sea with
   the ten Commandements, but scrap'd one out of the Table

2.Gent. Thou shalt not Steale?

Luc. I, that he raz'd

1.Gent. Why? 'twas a commandement, to command the Captaine and all the rest from their functions: they put forth to steale: There's not a Souldier of vs all, that in the thanks-giuing before meate, do rallish the petition well, that praies for peace

2.Gent. I neuer heard any Souldier dislike it

Luc. I beleeue thee: for I thinke thou neuer was't where Grace was said

2.Gent. No? a dozen times at least

1.Gent. What? In meeter?
Luc. In any proportion: or in any language

1.Gent. I thinke, or in any Religion

Luc. I, why not? Grace, is Grace, despight of all controuersie: as for example; Thou thy selfe art a wicked villaine, despight of all Grace

1.Gent. Well: there went but a paire of sheeres betweene vs

Luc. I grant: as there may betweene the Lists, and the Veluet. Thou art the List

1.Gent. And thou the Veluet; thou art good veluet; thou'rt a three pild-peece I warrant thee: I had as liefe be a Lyst of an English Kersey, as be pil'd, as thou art pil'd, for a French Veluet. Do I speake feelingly now?
Luc. I thinke thou do'st: and indeed with most painfull feeling of thy speech: I will, out of thine owne confession, learne to begin thy health; but, whilst I liue forget to drinke after thee

1.Gen. I think I haue done my selfe wrong, haue I not?
2.Gent. Yes, that thou hast; whether thou art tainted, or free.

Enter Bawde.

Luc. Behold, behold, where Madam Mitigation comes.
    I haue purchas'd as many diseases vnder her Roofe,
    As come to
2.Gent. To what, I pray?
Luc. Iudge

2.Gent. To three thousand Dollours a yeare

1.Gent. I, and more

Luc. A French crowne more

1.Gent. Thou art alwayes figuring diseases in me; but thou art full of error,
I am sound

Luc. Nay, not (as one would say) healthy: but so sound, as things that are
    hollow; thy bones are hollow; Impiety has made a feast of thee

1.Gent. How now, which of your hips has the most profound Ciatica?
Bawd. Well, well: there's one yonder arrested, and carried to prison, was
    worth fiue thousand of you all

2.Gent. Who's that I pray'thee?
Bawd. Marry Sir, that's Claudio, Signior Claudio

1.Gent. Claudio to prison? 'tis not so

Bawd. Nay, but I know 'tis so: I saw him arrested: saw him carried away:
    and which is more, within these three daies his head to be chop'd
    off

Luc. But, after all this fooling, I would not haue it so:
    Art thou sure of this?
Bawd. I am too sure of it: and it is for getting Madam Iulietta with childe

Luc. Beleeue me this may be: he promis'd to meete me two howres since,
    and he was euer precise in promise keeping

2.Gent. Besides you know, it drawes somthing neere to the speech we had to such a purpose

1.Gent. But most of all agreeing with the proclamatio[n]

Luc. Away: let's goe learne the truth of it.

Enter.

Bawd. Thus, what with the war; what with the sweat, what with the gallowes, and what with pouerty, I am Custom-shrunke. How now? what's the newes with you.

Enter Clowne.

Clo. Yonder man is carried to prison

Baw. Well: what has he done?
Clo. A Woman

Baw. But what's his offence?
Clo. Groping for Trowts, in a peculiar Riuer

Baw. What? is there a maid with child by him?
Clo. No: but there's a woman with maid by him: you haue not heard of the proclamation, haue you?
Baw. What proclamation, man?
Clow. All howses in the Suburbs of Vienna must bee pluck'd downe

Bawd. And what shall become of those in the Citie?
Clow. They shall stand for seed: they had gon down to, but that a wise Burger put in for them

Bawd. But shall all our houses of resort in the Suburbs be puld downe?
Clow. To the ground, Mistris

Bawd. Why heere's a change indeed in the Commonwealth: what shall become of me?

Clow. Come: feare not you; good Counsellors lacke no Clients: though you change your place, you neede not change your Trade: Ile bee your Tapster still; courage, there will bee pitty taken on you; you that haue worne your eyes almost out in the seruice, you will bee considered

Bawd. What's to doe heere, Thomas Tapster? let's withdraw?

Clo. Here comes Signior Claudio, led by the Prouost to prison: and there's Madam Iuliet.

Exeunt.

Scena Tertia.

Enter Prouost, Claudio, Iuliet, Officers, Lucio, & 2.Gent.

Cla. Fellow, why do'st thou show me thus to th' world?
  Beare me to prison, where I am committed

Pro. I do it not in euill disposition,
  But from Lord Angelo by speciall charge

Clau. Thus can the demy-god (Authority)
  Make vs pay downe, for our offence, by waight
  The words of heauen; on whom it will, it will,
  On whom it will not (soe) yet still 'tis iust

Luc. Why how now Claudio? whence comes this restraint

Cla. From too much liberty, (my Lucio) Liberty
  As surfet is the father of much fast,
  So euery Scope by the immoderate vse
  Turnes to restraint: Our Natures doe pursue
  Like Rats that rauyn downe their proper Bane,
  A thirsty euill, and when we drinke, we die

Luc. If I could speake so wisely vnder an arrest, I would send for certaine of my Creditors: and yet, to say the truth, I had as lief haue the foppery of freedome, as the mortality of imprisonment: what's thy offence, Claudio?
Cla. What (but to speake of) would offend againe

Luc. What, is't murder?
Cla. No

Luc. Lecherie?
Cla. Call it so

Pro. Away, Sir, you must goe

Cla. One word, good friend:
Lucio, a word with you

Luc. A hundred:
If they'll doe you any good: Is Lechery so look'd after?
Cla. Thus stands it with me: vpon a true contract
I got possession of Iulietas bed,
You know the Lady, she is fast my wife,
Saue that we doe the denunciation lacke
Of outward Order. This we came not to,
Onely for propogation of a Dowre
Remaining in the Coffer of her friends,
From whom we thought it meet to hide our Loue
Till Time had made them for vs. But it chances
The stealth of our most mutuall entertainment
With Character too grosse, is writ on Iuliet

Luc. With childe, perhaps?
Cla. Vnhappely, euen so.
And the new Deputie, now for the Duke,
Whether it be the fault and glimpse of newnes,
Or whether that the body publique, be
A horse whereon the Gouernor doth ride,

Who newly in the Seate, that it may know
He can command; lets it strait feele the spur:
Whether the Tirranny be in his place,
Or in his Eminence that fills it vp
I stagger in: But this new Gouernor
Awakes me all the inrolled penalties
Which haue (like vn-scowr'd Armor) hung by th' wall
So long, that ninteene Zodiacks haue gone round,
And none of them beene worne; and for a name
Now puts the drowsie and neglected Act
Freshly on me: 'tis surely for a name

Luc. I warrant it is: And thy head stands so tickle on thy shoulders, that a milke-maid, if she be in loue, may sigh it off: Send after the Duke, and appeale to him

Cla. I haue done so, but hee's not to be found.
I pre'thee (Lucio) doe me this kinde seruice:
This day, my sister should the Cloyster enter,
And there receiue her approbation.
Acquaint her with the danger of my state,
Implore her, in my voice, that she make friends
To the strict deputie: bid her selfe assay him,
I haue great hope in that: for in her youth
There is a prone and speechlesse dialect,
Such as moue men: beside, she hath prosperous Art
When she will play with reason, and discourse,
And well she can perswade

Luc. I pray shee may; aswell for the encouragement of the like, which else would stand vnder greeuous imposition: as for the enioying of thy life, who I would be sorry should bee thus foolishly lost, at a game of ticketacke: Ile to her

Cla. I thanke you good friend Lucio

Luc. Within two houres

Cla. Come Officer, away.

Exeunt.

Scena Quarta.

Enter Duke and Frier Thomas.

Duk. No: holy Father, throw away that thought,
    Beleeue not that the dribling dart of Loue
    Can pierce a compleat bosome: why, I desire thee
    To giue me secret harbour, hath a purpose
    More graue, and wrinkled, then the aimes, and ends
    Of burning youth

Fri. May your Grace speake of it?
Duk. My holy Sir, none better knowes then you
    How I haue euer lou'd the life remoued
    And held in idle price, to haunt assemblies
    Where youth, and cost, witlesse brauery keepes.
    I haue deliuerd to Lord Angelo
    (A man of stricture and firme abstinence)
    My absolute power, and place here in Vienna,
    And he supposes me trauaild to Poland,
    (For so I haue strewd it in the common eare)
    And so it is receiu'd: Now (pious Sir)
    You will demand of me, why I do this

Fri. Gladly, my Lord

Duk. We haue strict Statutes, and most biting Laws,
    (The needfull bits and curbes to headstrong weedes,)
    Which for this foureteene yeares, we haue let slip,
    Euen like an ore-growne Lyon in a Caue
    That goes not out to prey: Now, as fond Fathers,

> Hauing bound vp the threatning twigs of birch,
> Onely to sticke it in their childrens sight,
> For terror, not to vse: in time the rod
> More mock'd, then fear'd: so our Decrees,
> Dead to infliction, to themselues are dead,
> And libertie, plucks Iustice by the nose;
> The Baby beates the Nurse, and quite athwart
> Goes all decorum

Fri. It rested in your Grace
> To vnloose this tyde-vp Iustice, when you pleas'd:
> And it in you more dreadfull would haue seem'd
> Then in Lord Angelo

Duk. I doe feare: too dreadfull:
> Sith 'twas my fault, to giue the people scope,
> 'Twould be my tirrany to strike and gall them,
> For what I bid them doe: For, we bid this be done
> When euill deedes haue their permissiue passe,
> And not the punishment: therefore indeede (my father)
> I haue on Angelo impos'd the office,
> Who may in th' ambush of my name, strike home,
> And yet, my nature neuer in the sight
> To do in slander: And to behold his sway
> I will, as 'twere a brother of your Order,
> Visit both Prince, and People: Therefore I pre'thee
> Supply me with the habit, and instruct me
> How I may formally in person beare
> Like a true Frier: Moe reasons for this action
> At our more leysure, shall I render you;
> Onely, this one: Lord Angelo is precise,
> Stands at a guard with Enuie: scarce confesses
> That his blood flowes: or that his appetite
> Is more to bread then stone: hence shall we see
> If power change purpose: what our Seemers be.

Enter.

Measure, For Measure

Scena Quinta.

Enter Isabell and Francisca a Nun.

Isa. And haue you Nuns no farther priuiledges?
Nun. Are not these large enough?
Isa. Yes truely; I speake not as desiring more,
    But rather wishing a more strict restraint
    Vpon the Sisterhood, the Votarists of Saint Clare.

Lucio within.

Luc. Hoa? peace be in this place

Isa. Who's that which cals?
Nun. It is a mans voice: gentle Isabella
    Turne you the key, and know his businesse of him;
    You may; I may not: you are yet vnsworne:
    When you haue vowd, you must not speake with men,
    But in the presence of the Prioresse;
    Then if you speake, you must not show your face;
    Or if you show your face, you must not speake.
    He cals againe: I pray you answere him

Isa. Peace and prosperitie: who is't that cals?
Luc. Haile Virgin, (if you be) as those cheeke-Roses
    Proclaime you are no lesse: can you so steed me,
    As bring me to the sight of Isabella,
    A Nouice of this place, and the faire Sister
    To her vnhappie brother Claudio?
Isa. Why her vnhappy Brother? Let me aske,
    The rather for I now must make you know
    I am that Isabella, and his Sister

Luc. Gentle & faire: your Brother kindly greets you;
    Not to be weary with you; he's in prison

Isa. Woe me; for what?
Luc. For that, which if my selfe might be his Iudge,
    He should receiue his punishment, in thankes:
    He hath got his friend with childe

Isa. Sir, make me not your storie

Luc. 'Tis true; I would not, though 'tis my familiar sin,
    With Maids to seeme the Lapwing, and to iest
    Tongue, far from heart: play with all Virgins so:
    I hold you as a thing en-skied, and sainted,
    By your renouncement, an imortall spirit
    And to be talk'd with in sincerity,
    As with a Saint

Isa. You doe blaspheme the good, in mocking me

Luc. Doe not beleeue it: fewnes, and truth; tis thus,
    Your brother, and his louer haue embrac'd;
    As those that feed, grow full: as blossoming Time
    That from the seednes, the bare fallow brings
    To teeming foyson: euen so her plenteous wombe
    Expresseth his full Tilth, and husbandry

Isa. Some one with childe by him? my cosen Iuliet?
Luc. Is she your cosen?
Isa. Adoptedly, as schoole-maids change their names
    By vaine, though apt affection

Luc. She it is

Isa. Oh, let him marry her

Luc. This is the point.
    The Duke is very strangely gone from hence;
    Bore many gentlemen (my selfe being one)

In hand, and hope of action: but we doe learne,
By those that know the very Nerues of State,
His giuing-out, were of an infinite distance
From his true meant designe: vpon his place,
(And with full line of his authority)
Gouernes Lord Angelo; A man, whose blood
Is very snow-broth: one, who neuer feeles
The wanton stings, and motions of the sence;
But doth rebate, and blunt his naturall edge
With profits of the minde: Studie, and fast
He (to giue feare to vse, and libertie,
Which haue, for long, run-by the hideous law,
As Myce, by Lyons) hath pickt out an act,
Vnder whose heauy sence, your brothers life
Fals into forfeit: he arrests him on it,
And followes close the rigor of the Statute
To make him an example: all hope is gone,
Vnlesse you haue the grace, by your faire praier
To soften Angelo: And that's my pith of businesse
'Twixt you, and your poore brother

Isa. Doth he so,
     Seeke his life?
Luc. Has censur'd him already,
     And as I heare, the Prouost hath a warrant
     For's execution

Isa. Alas: what poore
     Abilitie's in me, to doe him good

Luc. Assay the powre you haue

Isa. My power? alas, I doubt

Luc. Our doubts are traitors
     And makes vs loose the good we oft might win,
     By fearing to attempt: Goe to Lord Angelo

And let him learne to know, when Maidens sue
Men giue like gods: but when they weepe and kneele,
All their petitions, are as freely theirs
As they themselues would owe them

Isa. Ile see what I can doe

Luc. But speedily

Isa. I will about it strait;
No longer staying, but to giue the Mother
Notice of my affaire: I humbly thanke you:
Commend me to my brother: soone at night
Ile send him certaine word of my successe

Luc. I take my leaue of you

Isa. Good sir, adieu.

Exeunt.

ACTUS SECUNDUS

Scoena Prima.

Enter Angelo, Escalus, and seruants, Iustice.

Ang. We must not make a scar-crow of the Law,
    Setting it vp to feare the Birds of prey,
    And let it keepe one shape, till custome make it
    Their pearch, and not their terror

Esc. I, but yet
    Let vs be keene, and rather cut a little
    Then fall, and bruise to death: alas, this gentleman
    Whom I would saue, had a most noble father,
    Let but your honour know
    (Whom I beleeue to be most strait in vertue)
    That in the working of your owne affections,
    Had time coheard with Place, or place with wishing,
    Or that the resolute acting of our blood
    Could haue attaind th' effect of your owne purpose,
    Whether you had not sometime in your life

       Er'd in this point, which now you censure him,
       And puld the Law vpon you

Ang. 'Tis one thing to be tempted (Escalus)
      Another thing to fall: I not deny
      The Iury passing on the Prisoners life
      May in the sworne-twelue haue a thiefe, or two
      Guiltier then him they try; what's open made to Iustice,
      That Iustice ceizes; What knowes the Lawes
      That theeues do passe on theeues? 'Tis very pregnant,
      The Iewell that we finde, we stoope, and take't,
      Because we see it; but what we doe not see,
      We tread vpon, and neuer thinke of it.
      You may not so extenuate his offence,
      For I haue had such faults; but rather tell me
      When I, that censure him, do so offend,
      Let mine owne Iudgement patterne out my death,
      And nothing come in partiall. Sir, he must dye.

Enter Prouost.

Esc. Be it as your wisedome will

Ang. Where is the Prouost?
Pro. Here if it like your honour

Ang. See that Claudio
      Be executed by nine to morrow morning,
      Bring him his Confessor, let him be prepar'd,
      For that's the vtmost of his pilgrimage

Esc. Well: heauen forgiue him; and forgiue vs all:
      Some rise by sinne, and some by vertue fall:
      Some run from brakes of Ice, and answere none,
      And some condemned for a fault alone.

Enter Elbow, Froth, Clowne, Officers.

Elb. Come, bring them away: if these be good people in a Common-weale, that doe nothing but vse their abuses in common houses, I know no law: bring them away

Ang. How now Sir, what's your name? And what's the matter?
Elb. If it please your honour, I am the poore Dukes Constable, and my name is Elbow; I doe leane vpon Iustice Sir, and doe bring in here before your good honor, two notorious Benefactors

Ang. Benefactors? Well: What Benefactors are they?
  Are they not Malefactors?
Elb. If it please your honour, I know not well what they are: But precise villaines they are, that I am sure of, and void of all prophanation in the world, that good Christians ought to haue

Esc. This comes off well: here's a wise Officer

Ang. Goe to: What quality are they of? Elbow is your name?
  Why do'st thou not speake Elbow?
Clo. He cannot Sir: he's out at Elbow

Ang. What are you Sir?
Elb. He Sir: a Tapster Sir: parcell Baud: one that serues a bad woman: whose house Sir was (as they say) pluckt downe in the Suborbs: and now shee professes a hot-house; which, I thinke is a very ill house too

Esc. How know you that?
Elb. My wife Sir? whom I detest before heauen, and your honour

Esc. How? thy wife?
Elb. I Sir: whom I thanke heauen is an honest woman

Esc. Do'st thou detest her therefore?
Elb. I say sir, I will detest my selfe also, as well as she, that this house, if it be not a Bauds house, it is pitty of her life, for it is a naughty house

Esc. How do'st thou know that, Constable?
Elb. Marry sir, by my wife, who, if she had bin a woman Cardinally giuen, might haue bin accus'd in fornication, adultery, and all vncleanlinesse there

Esc. By the womans meanes?
Elb. I sir, by Mistris Ouerdons meanes: but as she spit in his face, so she defide him

Clo. Sir, if it please your honor, this is not so

Elb. Proue it before these varlets here, thou honorable man, proue it

Esc. Doe you heare how he misplaces?
Clo. Sir, she came in great with childe: and longing (sauing your honors reuerence) for stewd prewyns; sir, we had but two in the house, which at that very distant time stood, as it were in a fruit dish (a dish of some three pence; your honours haue seene such dishes) they are not China-dishes, but very good dishes

Esc. Go too: go too: no matter for the dish sir

Clo. No indeede sir not of a pin; you are therein in the right: but, to the point: As I say, this Mistris Elbow, being (as I say) with childe, and being great bellied, and longing (as I said) for prewyns: and hauing but two in the dish (as I said) Master Froth here, this very man, hauing eaten the rest (as I said) & (as I say) paying for them very honestly: for, as you know Master Froth, I could not giue you three pence againe

Fro. No indeede

Clo. Very well: you being then (if you be remembred) cracking the stones of the foresaid prewyns

Fro. I, so I did indeede

Clo. Why, very well: I telling you then (if you be remembred) that such a one, and such a one, were past cure of the thing you wot of, vnlesse they kept very good diet, as I told you

Fro. All this is true

Clo. Why very well then

Esc. Come: you are a tedious foole: to the purpose: what was done to Elbowes wife, that hee hath cause to complaine of? Come me to what was done to her

Clo. Sir, your honor cannot come to that yet

Esc. No sir, nor I meane it not

Clo. Sir, but you shall come to it, by your honours leaue: And I beseech you, looke into Master Froth here sir, a man of foure-score pound a yeare; whose father died at Hallowmas: Was't not at Hallowmas Master Froth?
Fro. Allhallond-Eue

Clo. Why very well: I hope here be truthes: he Sir, sitting (as I say) in a lower chaire, Sir, 'twas in the bunch of Grapes, where indeede you haue a delight to sit, haue you not?
Fro. I haue so, because it is an open roome, and good for winter

Clo. Why very well then: I hope here be truthes

Ang. This will last out a night in Russia When nights are longest there: Ile take my leaue, And leaue you to the hearing of the cause; Hoping youle finde good cause to whip them all.

Enter.

Esc. I thinke no lesse: good morrow to your Lordship. Now Sir, come on: What was done to Elbowes wife, once more?

Clo. Once Sir? there was nothing done to her once

Elb. I beseech you Sir, aske him what this man did to my wife

Clo. I beseech your honor, aske me

Esc. Well sir, what did this Gentleman to her?
Clo. I beseech you sir, looke in this Gentlemans face: good Master Froth looke vpon his honor; 'tis for a good purpose: doth your honor marke his face?
Esc. I sir, very well

Clo. Nay, I beseech you marke it well

Esc. Well, I doe so

Clo. Doth your honor see any harme in his face?
Esc. Why no

Clo. Ile be supposd vpon a booke, his face is the worst thing about him: good then: if his face be the worst thing about him, how could Master Froth doe the Constables wife any harme? I would know that of your honour

Esc. He's in the right (Constable) what say you to it?
Elb. First, and it like you, the house is a respected house; next, this is a respected fellow; and his Mistris is a respected woman

Clo. By this hand Sir, his wife is a more respected person then any of vs all

Elb. Varlet, thou lyest; thou lyest wicked varlet: the time is yet to come that shee was euer respected with man, woman, or childe

Clo. Sir, she was respected with him, before he married with her

Esc. Which is the wiser here; Iustice or Iniquitie? Is this true?

Elb. O thou caytiffe: O thou varlet: O thou wicked Hanniball; I respected with her, before I was married to her? If euer I was respected with her, or she with me, let not your worship thinke mee the poore Dukes Officer: proue this, thou wicked Hanniball, or ile haue mine action of battry on thee

Esc. If he tooke you a box o'th' eare, you might haue your action of slander too

Elb. Marry I thanke your good worship for it: what is't your Worships pleasure I shall doe with this wicked Caitiffe?
Esc. Truly Officer, because he hath some offences in him, that thou wouldst discouer, if thou couldst, let him continue in his courses, till thou knowst what they are

Elb. Marry I thanke your worship for it: Thou seest thou wicked varlet now, what's come vpon thee. Thou art to continue now thou Varlet, thou art to continue

Esc. Where were you borne, friend?
Froth. Here in Vienna, Sir

Esc. Are you of fourescore pounds a yeere?
Froth. Yes, and't please you sir

Esc. So: what trade are you of, sir?
Clo. A Tapster, a poore widdowes Tapster

Esc. Your Mistris name?
Clo. Mistris Ouerdon

Esc. Hath she had any more then one husband?
Clo. Nine, sir: Ouerdon by the last

Esc. Nine? come hether to me, Master Froth; Master Froth, I would not haue you acquainted with Tapsters; they will draw you Master Froth, and you wil hang them: get you gon, and let me heare no more of you

Fro. I thanke your worship: for mine owne part, I neuer come into any roome in a Tap-house, but I am drawne in

Esc. Well: no more of it Master Froth: farewell:
   Come you hether to me, Mr. Tapster: what's your name Mr. Tapster?
Clo. Pompey

Esc. What else?
Clo. Bum, Sir

Esc. Troth, and your bum is the greatest thing about you, so that in the beastliest sence, you are Pompey the great; Pompey, you are partly a bawd, Pompey; howsoeuer you colour it in being a Tapster, are you not? come, tell me true, it shall be the better for you

Clo. Truly sir, I am a poore fellow that would liue

Esc. How would you liue Pompey? by being a bawd? what doe you thinke of the trade Pompey? is it a lawfull trade?
Clo. If the Law would allow it, sir

Esc. But the Law will not allow it Pompey; nor it shall not be allowed in Vienna

Clo. Do's your Worship meane to geld and splay all the youth of the City?
Esc. No, Pompey

Clo. Truely Sir, in my poore opinion they will too't then: if your worship will take order for the drabs and the knaues, you need not to feare the bawds

Esc. There is pretty orders beginning I can tell you: It is but heading, and hanging

Clo. If you head, and hang all that offend that way but for ten yeare together; you'll be glad to giue out a Commission for more heads: if this law hold in Vienna ten yeare, ile rent the fairest house in it after three pence a Bay: if you liue to see this come to passe, say Pompey told you so

Esc. Thanke you good Pompey; and in requitall of your prophesie, harke you: I aduise you let me not finde you before me againe vpon any complaint whatsoeuer; no, not for dwelling where you doe: if I doe Pompey, I shall beat you to your Tent, and proue a shrewd Cæsar to you: in plaine dealing Pompey, I shall haue you whipt; so for this time, Pompey, fare you well

Clo. I thanke your Worship for your good counsell; but I shall follow it as the flesh and fortune shall better determine. Whip me? no, no, let Carman whip his Iade, The valiant heart's not whipt out of his trade.

Enter.

Esc. Come hether to me, Master Elbow: come hither Master Constable: how long haue you bin in this place of Constable?
Elb. Seuen yeere, and a halfe sir

Esc. I thought by the readinesse in the office, you had continued in it some time: you say seauen yeares together

Elb. And a halfe sir

Esc. Alas, it hath beene great paines to you: they do you wrong to put you so oft vpon't. Are there not men in your Ward sufficient to serue it?
Elb. 'Faith sir, few of any wit in such matters: as they are chosen, they are glad to choose me for them; I do it for some peece of money, and goe through with all

Esc. Looke you bring mee in the names of some sixe or seuen, the most sufficient of your parish

Elb. To your Worships house sir?
Esc. To my house: fare you well: what's a clocke, thinke you?

Iust. Eleuen, Sir

Esc. I pray you home to dinner with me

Iust. I humbly thanke you

Esc. It grieues me for the death of Claudio
    But there's no remedie:
Iust. Lord Angelo is seuere

Esc. It is but needfull.
    Mercy is not it selfe, that oft lookes so,
    Pardon is still the nurse of second woe:
    But yet, poore Claudio; there is no remedie.
    Come Sir.

Exeunt.

Scena Secunda.

Enter Prouost, Seruant.

Ser. Hee's hearing of a Cause; he will come straight,
    I'le tell him of you

Pro. 'Pray you doe; Ile know
    His pleasure, may be he will relent; alas
    He hath but as offended in a dreame,
    All Sects, all Ages smack of this vice, and he
    To die for't?

Enter Angelo.

Ang. Now, what's the matter Prouost?
Pro. Is it your will Claudio shall die to morrow?

Ang. Did not I tell thee yea? hadst thou not order?
    Why do'st thou aske againe?
Pro. Lest I might be too rash:
    Vnder your good correction I haue seene
    When after execution, Iudgement hath
    Repented ore his doome

Ang. Goe to; let that be mine,
    Doe you your office, or giue vp your Place,
    And you shall well be spar'd

Pro. I craue your Honours pardon:
    What shall be done Sir, with the groaning Iuliet?
    Shee's very neere her howre

Ang. Dispose of her
    To some more fitter place; and that with speed

Ser. Here is the sister of the man condemn'd,
    Desires accesse to you

Ang. Hath he a Sister?
Pro. I my good Lord, a very vertuous maid,
    And to be shortlie of a Sister-hood,
    If not alreadie

Ang. Well: let her be admitted,
    See you the Fornicatresse be remou'd,
    Let her haue needfull, but not lauish meanes,
    There shall be order for't.

Enter Lucio and Isabella.

Pro. 'Saue your Honour

Ang. Stay a little while: y'are welcome: what's your will?

Isab. I am a wofull Sutor to your Honour,
    'Please but your Honor heare me

Ang. Well: what's your suite

Isab. There is a vice that most I doe abhorre,
    And most desire should meet the blow of Iustice;
    For which I would not plead, but that I must,
    For which I must not plead, but that I am
    At warre, twixt will, and will not

Ang. Well: the matter?
Isab. I haue a brother is condemn'd to die,
    I doe beseech you let it be his fault,
    And not my brother

Pro. Heauen giue thee mouing graces

Ang. Condemne the fault, and not the actor of it,
    Why euery fault's condemnd ere it be done:
    Mine were the verie Cipher of a Function
    To fine the faults, whose fine stands in record,
    And let goe by the Actor

Isab. Oh iust, but seuere Law:
    I had a brother then; heauen keepe your honour

Luc. Giue't not ore so: to him againe, entreat him,
    Kneele downe before him, hang vpon his gowne,
    You are too cold: if you should need a pin,
    You could not with more tame a tongue desire it:
    To him, I say

Isab. Must he needs die?
Ang. Maiden, no remedie

Isab. Yes: I doe thinke that you might pardon him,
    And neither heauen, nor man grieue at the mercy

Ang. I will not doe't

Isab. But can you if you would?
Ang. Looke what I will not, that I cannot doe

Isab. But might you doe't & do the world no wrong
    If so your heart were touch'd with that remorse,
    As mine is to him?
Ang. Hee's sentenc'd, tis too late

Luc. You are too cold

Isab. Too late? why no: I that doe speak a word
    May call it againe: well, beleeue this
    No ceremony that to great ones longs,
    Not the Kings Crowne; nor the deputed sword,
    The Marshalls Truncheon, nor the Iudges Robe
    Become them with one halfe so good a grace
    As mercie does: If he had bin as you, and you as he,
    You would haue slipt like him, but he like you
    Would not haue beene so sterne

Ang. Pray you be gone

Isab. I would to heauen I had your potencie,
    And you were Isabell: should it then be thus?
    No: I would tell what 'twere to be a Iudge,
    And what a prisoner

Luc. I, touch him: there's the veine

Ang. Your Brother is a forfeit of the Law,
    And you but waste your words

Isab. Alas, alas:
    Why all the soules that were, were forfeit once,
    And he that might the vantage best haue tooke,

Found out the remedie: how would you be,
If he, which is the top of Iudgement, should
But iudge you, as you are? Oh, thinke on that,
And mercie then will breathe within your lips
Like man new made

Ang. Be you content, (faire Maid)
It is the Law, not I, condemne your brother,
Were he my kinsman, brother, or my sonne,
It should be thus with him: he must die to morrow

Isab. To morrow? oh, that's sodaine,
Spare him, spare him:
Hee's not prepar'd for death; euen for our kitchins
We kill the fowle of season: shall we serue heauen
With lesse respect then we doe minister
To our grosse-selues? good, good my Lord, bethink you;
Who is it that hath di'd for this offence?
There's many haue committed it

Luc. I, well said

Ang. The Law hath not bin dead, thogh it hath slept
Those many had not dar'd to doe that euill
If the first, that did th' Edict infringe
Had answer'd for his deed. Now 'tis awake,
Takes note of what is done, and like a Prophet
Lookes in a glasse that shewes what future euils
Either now, or by remissenesse, new conceiu'd,
And so in progresse to be hatch'd, and borne,
Are now to haue no successiue degrees,
But here they liue to end

Isab. Yet shew some pittie

Ang. I shew it most of all, when I show Iustice;
For then I pittie those I doe not know,

              Which a dismis'd offence, would after gaule
              And doe him right, that answering one foule wrong
              Liues not to act another. Be satisfied;
              Your Brother dies to morrow; be content

Isab. So you must be y first that giues this sentence,
       And hee, that suffers: Oh, it is excellent
       To haue a Giants strength: but it is tyrannous
       To vse it like a Giant

Luc. That's well said

Isab. Could great men thunder
       As Ioue himselfe do's, Ioue would neuer be quiet,
       For euery pelting petty Officer
       Would vse his heauen for thunder;
       Nothing but thunder: Mercifull heauen,
       Thou rather with thy sharpe and sulpherous bolt
       Splits the vn-wedgable and gnarled Oke,
       Then the soft Mertill: But man, proud man,
       Drest in a little briefe authoritie,
       Most ignorant of what he's most assur'd,
       (His glassie Essence) like an angry Ape
       Plaies such phantastique tricks before high heauen,
       As makes the Angels weepe: who with our spleenes,
       Would all themselues laugh mortall

Luc. Oh, to him, to him wench: he will relent,
      Hee's comming: I perceiue't

Pro. Pray heauen she win him

Isab. We cannot weigh our brother with our selfe,
       Great men may iest with Saints: tis wit in them,
       But in the lesse fowle prophanation

Luc. Thou'rt i'th right (Girle) more o'that

Isab. That in the Captaine's but a chollericke word,
    Which in the Souldier is flat blasphemie

Luc. Art auis'd o'that? more on't

Ang. Why doe you put these sayings vpon me?
Isab. Because Authoritie, though it erre like others,
    Hath yet a kinde of medicine in it selfe
    That skins the vice o'th top; goe to your bosome,
    Knock there, and aske your heart what it doth know
    That's like my brothers fault: if it confesse
    A naturall guiltinesse, such as is his,
    Let it not sound a thought vpon your tongue
    Against my brothers life

Ang. Shee speakes, and 'tis such sence
    That my Sence breeds with it; fare you well

Isab. Gentle my Lord, turne backe

Ang. I will bethinke me: come againe to morrow

Isa. Hark, how Ile bribe you: good my Lord turn back

Ang. How? bribe me?
    Is. I, with such gifts that heauen shall share with you

Luc. You had mar'd all else

Isab. Not with fond Sickles of the tested-gold,
    Or Stones, whose rate are either rich, or poore
    As fancie values them: but with true prayers,
    That shall be vp at heauen, and enter there
    Ere Sunne rise: prayers from preserued soules,
    From fasting Maides, whose mindes are dedicate
    To nothing temporall

Ang. Well: come to me to morrow

Luc. Goe to: 'tis well; away

Isab. Heauen keepe your honour safe

Ang. Amen.
    For I am that way going to temptation,
    Where prayers crosse

Isab. At what hower to morrow,
    Shall I attend your Lordship?
Ang. At any time 'fore-noone

Isab. 'Saue your Honour

Ang. From thee: euen from thy vertue.
    What's this? what's this? is this her fault, or mine?
    The Tempter, or the Tempted, who sins most? ha?
    Not she: nor doth she tempt: but it is I,
    That, lying by the Violet in the Sunne,
    Doe as the Carrion do's, not as the flowre,
    Corrupt with vertuous season: Can it be,
    That Modesty may more betray our Sence
    Then womans lightnesse? hauing waste ground enough,
    Shall we desire to raze the Sanctuary
    And pitch our euils there? oh fie, fie, fie:
    What dost thou? or what art thou Angelo?
    Dost thou desire her fowly, for those things
    That make her good? oh, let her brother liue:
    Theeues for their robbery haue authority,
    When Iudges steale themselues: what, doe I loue her,
    That I desire to heare her speake againe?
    And feast vpon her eyes? what is't I dreame on?
    Oh cunning enemy, that to catch a Saint,
    With Saints dost bait thy hooke: most dangerous

Is that temptation, that doth goad vs on
To sinne, in louing vertue: neuer could the Strumpet
With all her double vigor, Art, and Nature
Once stir my temper: but this vertuous Maid
Subdues me quite: Euer till now
When men were fond, I smild, and wondred how.

Enter.

Scena Tertia.

Enter Duke and Prouost.

Duke. Haile to you, Prouost, so I thinke you are

Pro. I am the Prouost: whats your will, good Frier?
Duke. Bound by my charity, and my blest order,
    I come to visite the afflicted spirits
    Here in the prison: doe me the common right
    To let me see them: and to make me know
    The nature of their crimes, that I may minister
    To them accordingly

Pro. I would do more then that, if more were needfull

Enter Iuliet.

Looke here comes one: a Gentlewoman of mine,
Who falling in the flawes of her owne youth,
Hath blisterd her report: She is with childe,
And he that got it, sentenc'd: a yong man,
More fit to doe another such offence,
Then dye for this

Duk. When must he dye?
Pro. As I do thinke to morrow.
    I haue prouided for you, stay a while
    And you shall be conducted

Duk. Repent you (faire one) of the sin you carry?
Iul. I doe; and beare the shame most patiently

Du. Ile teach you how you shal araign your conscie[n]ce
　　And try your penitence, if it be sound,
　　Or hollowly put on

Iul. Ile gladly learne

Duk. Loue you the man that wrong'd you?
Iul. Yes, as I loue the woman that wrong'd him

Duk. So then it seemes your most offence full act
　　Was mutually committed

Iul. Mutually

Duk. Then was your sin of heauier kinde then his

Iul. I doe confesse it, and repent it (Father.)
Duk. 'Tis meet so (daughter) but least you do repent
　　As that the sin hath brought you to this shame,
　　Which sorrow is alwaies toward our selues, not heauen,
　　Showing we would not spare heauen, as we loue it,
　　But as we stand in feare

Iul. I doe repent me, as it is an euill,
　　And take the shame with ioy

Duke. There rest:
　　Your partner (as I heare) must die to morrow,
　　And I am going with instruction to him:
　　Grace goe with you, Benedicite.

Enter.

Iul. Must die to morrow? oh iniurious Loue
    That respits me a life, whose very comfort
    Is still a dying horror

Pro. 'Tis pitty of him.

Exeunt.

Scena Quarta.

Enter Angelo.

An. When I would pray, & think, I thinke, and pray
    To seuerall subiects: heauen hath my empty words,
    Whilst my Inuention, hearing not my Tongue,
    Anchors on Isabell: heauen in my mouth,
    As if I did but onely chew his name,
    And in my heart the strong and swelling euill
    Of my conception: the state whereon I studied
    Is like a good thing, being often read
    Growne feard, and tedious: yea, my Grauitie
    Wherein (let no man heare me) I take pride,
    Could I, with boote, change for an idle plume
    Which the ayre beats for vaine: oh place, oh forme,
    How often dost thou with thy case, thy habit
    Wrench awe from fooles, and tye the wiser soules
    To thy false seeming? Blood, thou art blood,
    Let's write good Angell on the Deuills horne
    'Tis not the Deuills Crest: how now? who's there?

Enter Seruant.

Ser. One Isabell, a Sister, desires accesse to you

Ang. Teach her the way: oh, heauens
    Why doe's my bloud thus muster to my heart,
    Making both it vnable for it selfe,

And dispossessing all my other parts
Of necessary fitnesse?
So play the foolish throngs with one that swounds,
Come all to help him, and so stop the ayre
By which hee should reuiue: and euen so
The generall subiect to a wel-wisht King
Quit their owne part, and in obsequious fondnesse
Crowd to his presence, where their vn-taught loue
Must needs appear offence: how now faire Maid.

Enter Isabella.

Isab. I am come to know your pleasure

An. That you might know it, wold much better please me,
    Then to demand what 'tis: your Brother cannot liue

Isab. Euen so: heauen keepe your Honor

Ang. Yet may he liue a while: and it may be
    As long as you, or I: yet he must die

Isab. Vnder your Sentence?
Ang. Yea

Isab. When, I beseech you: that in his Reprieue
    (Longer, or shorter) he may be so fitted
    That his soule sicken not

Ang. Ha? fie, these filthy vices: It were as good
    To pardon him, that hath from nature stolne
    A man already made, as to remit
    Their sawcie sweetnes, that do coyne heauens Image
    In stamps that are forbid: 'tis all as easie,
    Falsely to take away a life true made,
    As to put mettle in restrained meanes
    To make a false one

Isab. 'Tis set downe so in heauen, but not in earth

Ang. Say you so: then I shall poze you quickly.
  Which had you rather, that the most iust Law
  Now tooke your brothers life, and to redeeme him
  Giue vp your body to such sweet vncleannesse
  As she that he hath staind?
Isab. Sir, beleeue this.
  I had rather giue my body, then my soule

Ang. I talke not of your soule: our compel'd sins
  Stand more for number, then for accompt

Isab. How say you?
Ang. Nay Ile not warrant that: for I can speake
  Against the thing I say: Answere to this,
  I (now the voyce of the recorded Law)
  Pronounce a sentence on your Brothers life,
  Might there not be a charitie in sinne,
  To saue this Brothers life?
Isab. Please you to doo't,
  Ile take it as a perill to my soule,
  It is no sinne at all, but charitie

Ang. Pleas'd you to doo't, at perill of your soule
  Were equall poize of sinne, and charitie

Isab. That I do beg his life, if it be sinne
  Heauen let me beare it: you granting of my suit,
  If that be sin, Ile make it my Morne-praier,
  To haue it added to the faults of mine,
  And nothing of your answere

Ang. Nay, but heare me,
  Your sence pursues not mine: either you are ignorant,
  Or seeme so crafty; and that's not good

Isab. Let be ignorant, and in nothing good,
   But graciously to know I am no better

Ang. Thus wisdome wishes to appeare most bright,
   When it doth taxe it selfe: As these blacke Masques
   Proclaime an en-shield beauty ten times louder
   Then beauty could displaied: But marke me,
   To be receiued plaine, Ile speake more grosse:
   Your Brother is to dye

Isab. So

Ang. And his offence is so, as it appeares,
   Accountant to the Law, vpon that paine

Isab. True

Ang. Admit no other way to saue his life
   (As I subscribe not that, nor any other,
   But in the losse of question) that you, his Sister,
   Finding your selfe desir'd of such a person,
   Whose creadit with the Iudge, or owne great place,
   Could fetch your Brother from the Manacles
   Of the all-building-Law: and that there were
   No earthly meane to saue him, but that either
   You must lay downe the treasures of your body,
   To this supposed, or else to let him suffer:
   What would you doe?
Isab. As much for my poore Brother, as my selfe;
   That is: were I vnder the tearmes of death,
   Th' impression of keene whips, I'ld weare as Rubies,
   And strip my selfe to death, as to a bed,
   That longing haue bin sicke for, ere I'ld yeeld
   My body vp to shame

Ang. Then must your brother die

Isa. And 'twer the cheaper way:
   Better it were a brother dide at once,
   Then that a sister, by redeeming him
   Should die for euer

Ang. Were not you then as cruell as the Sentence,
   That you haue slander'd so?
Isa. Ignomie in ransome, and free pardon
   Are of two houses: lawfull mercie,
   Is nothing kin to fowle redemption

Ang. You seem'd of late to make the Law a tirant,
   And rather prou'd the sliding of your brother
   A merriment, then a vice

Isa. Oh pardon me my Lord, it oft fals out
   To haue, what we would haue,
   We speake not what we meane;
   I something do excuse the thing I hate,
   For his aduantage that I dearely loue

Ang. We are all fraile

Isa. Else let my brother die,
   If not a fedarie but onely he
   Owe, and succeed thy weaknesse

Ang. Nay, women are fraile too

Isa. I, as the glasses where they view themselues,
   Which are as easie broke as they make formes:
   Women? Helpe heauen; men their creation marre
   In profiting by them: Nay, call vs ten times fraile,
   For we are soft, as our complexions are,
   And credulous to false prints

Ang. I thinke it well:
    And from this testimonie of your owne sex
    (Since I suppose we are made to be no stronger
    Then faults may shake our frames) let me be bold;
    I do arrest your words. Be that you are,
    That is a woman; if you be more, you'r none.
    If you be one (as you are well exprest
    By all externall warrants) shew it now,
    By putting on the destin'd Liuerie

Isa. I haue no tongue but one; gentle my Lord,
    Let me entreate you speake the former language

Ang. Plainlie conceiue I loue you

Isa. My brother did loue Iuliet,
    And you tell me that he shall die for't

Ang. He shall not Isabell if you giue me loue

Isa. I know your vertue hath a licence in't,
    Which seemes a little fouler then it is,
    To plucke on others

Ang. Beleeue me on mine Honor,
    My words expresse my purpose

Isa. Ha? Little honor, to be much beleeu'd,
    And most pernitious purpose: Seeming, seeming.
    I will proclaime thee Angelo, looke for't.
    Signe me a present pardon for my brother,
    Or with an out-stretcht throate Ile tell the world aloud
    What man thou art

Ang. Who will beleeue thee Isabell?
    My vnsoild name, th' austeerenesse of my life,
    My vouch against you, and my place i'th State,

Will so your accusation ouer-weigh,
That you shall stifle in your owne report,
And smell of calumnie. I haue begun,
And now I giue my sensuall race, the reine,
Fit thy consent to my sharpe appetite,
Lay by all nicetie, and prolixious blushes
That banish what they sue for: Redeeme thy brother,
By yeelding vp thy bodie to my will,
Or else he must not onelie die the death,
But thy vnkindnesse shall his death draw out
To lingring sufferance: Answer me to morrow,
Or by the affection that now guides me most,
Ile proue a Tirant to him. As for you,
Say what you can; my false, ore-weighs your true.

Exit

Isa. To whom should I complaine? Did I tell this,
Who would beleeue me? O perilous mouthes
That beare in them, one and the selfesame tongue,
Either of condemnation, or approofe,
Bidding the Law make curtsie to their will,
Hooking both right and wrong to th' appetite,
To follow as it drawes. Ile to my brother,
Though he hath falne by prompture of the blood,
Yet hath he in him such a minde of Honor,
That had he twentie heads to tender downe
On twentie bloodie blockes, hee'ld yeeld them vp,
Before his sister should her bodie stoope
To such abhord pollution.
Then Isabell liue chaste, and brother die;
``More then our Brother, is our Chastitie.
Ile tell him yet of Angelo's request,
And fit his minde to death, for his soules rest.

Enter.

ACTUS TERTIUS

Scena Prima.

Enter Duke, Claudio, and Prouost.

Du. So then you hope of pardon from Lord Angelo?
Cla. The miserable haue no other medicine
    But onely hope: I'haue hope to liue, and am prepar'd to die

Duke. Be absolute for death: either death or life
    Shall thereby be the sweeter. Reason thus with life:
    If I do loose thee, I do loose a thing
    That none but fooles would keepe: a breath thou art,
    Seruile to all the skyie-influences
    That dost this habitation where thou keepst
    Hourely afflict: Meerely, thou art deaths foole,
    For him thou labourst by thy flight to shun,
    And yet runst toward him still. Thou art not noble,
    For all th' accommodations that thou bearst,
    Are nurst by basenesse: Thou'rt by no meanes valiant,
    For thou dost feare the soft and tender forke

Of a poore worme: thy best of rest is sleepe,
And that thou oft prouoakst, yet grosselie fearst
Thy death, which is no more. Thou art not thy selfe,
For thou exists on manie a thousand graines
That issue out of dust. Happie thou art not,
For what thou hast not, still thou striu'st to get,
And what thou hast forgetst. Thou art not certaine,
For thy complexion shifts to strange effects,
After the Moone: If thou art rich, thou'rt poore,
For like an Asse, whose backe with Ingots bowes;
Thou bearst thy heauie riches but a iournie,
And death vnloads thee; Friend hast thou none.
For thine owne bowels which do call thee, fire
The meere effusion of thy proper loines
Do curse the Gowt, Sapego, and the Rheume
For ending thee no sooner. Thou hast nor youth, nor age
But as it were an after-dinners sleepe
Dreaming on both, for all thy blessed youth
Becomes as aged, and doth begge the almes
Of palsied-Eld: and when thou art old, and rich
Thou hast neither heate, affection, limbe, nor beautie
To make thy riches pleasant: what's yet in this
That beares the name of life? Yet in this life
Lie hid moe thousand deaths; yet death we feare
That makes these oddes, all euen

Cla. I humblie thanke you.
  To sue to liue, I finde I seeke to die,
  And seeking death, finde life: Let it come on.

Enter Isabella.

Isab. What hoa? Peace heere; Grace, and good companie

Pro. Who's there? Come in, the wish deserues a welcome

Duke. Deere sir, ere long Ile visit you againe

Cla. Most holie Sir, I thanke you

Isa. My businesse is a word or two with Claudio

Pro. And verie welcom: looke Signior, here's your sister

Duke. Prouost, a word with you

Pro. As manie as you please

Duke. Bring them to heare me speak, where I may be conceal'd

Cla. Now sister, what's the comfort?
Isa. Why,
    As all comforts are: most good, most good indeede,
    Lord Angelo hauing affaires to heauen
    Intends you for his swift Ambassador,
    Where you shall be an euerlasting Leiger;
    Therefore your best appointment make with speed,
    To Morrow you set on

Clau. Is there no remedie?
Isa. None, but such remedie, as to saue a head
    To cleaue a heart in twaine:
Clau. But is there anie?
Isa. Yes brother, you may liue;
    There is a diuellish mercie in the Iudge,
    If you'l implore it, that will free your life,
    But fetter you till death

Cla. Perpetuall durance?
Isa. I iust, perpetuall durance, a restraint
    Through all the worlds vastiditie you had
    To a determin'd scope

Clau. But in what nature?

Isa. In such a one, as you consenting too't,
    Would barke your honor from that trunke you beare,
    And leaue you naked

Clau. Let me know the point

Isa. Oh, I do feare thee Claudio, and I quake,
    Least thou a feauorous life shouldst entertaine,
    And six or seuen winters more respect
    Then a perpetuall Honor. Dar'st thou die?
    The sence of death is most in apprehension,
    And the poore Beetle that we treade vpon
    In corporall sufferance, finds a pang as great,
    As when a Giant dies

Cla. Why giue you me this shame?
    Thinke you I can a resolution fetch
    From flowrie tendernesse? If I must die,
    I will encounter darknesse as a bride,
    And hugge it in mine armes

Isa. There spake my brother: there my fathers graue
    Did vtter forth a voice. Yes, thou must die:
    Thou art too noble, to conserue a life
    In base appliances. This outward sainted Deputie,
    Whose setled visage, and deliberate word
    Nips youth i'th head, and follies doth emmew
    As Falcon doth the Fowle, is yet a diuell:
    His filth within being cast, he would appeare
    A pond, as deepe as hell

Cla. The prenzie, Angelo?
Isa. Oh 'tis the cunning Liuerie of hell,
    The damnest bodie to inuest, and couer
    In prenzie gardes; dost thou thinke Claudio,
    If I would yeeld him my virginitie
    Thou might'st be freed?

Measure, For Measure

Cla. Oh heauens, it cannot be

Isa. Yes, he would giu't thee; from this rank offence
    So to offend him still. This night's the time
    That I should do what I abhorre to name,
    Or else thou diest to morrow

Clau. Thou shalt not do't

Isa. O, were it but my life,
    I'de throw it downe for your deliuerance
    As frankely as a pin

Clau. Thankes deere Isabell

Isa. Be readie Claudio, for your death to morrow

Clau. Yes. Has he affections in him,
    That thus can make him bite the Law by th' nose,
    When he would force it? Sure it is no sinne,
    Or of the deadly seuen it is the least

Isa. Which is the least?
Cla. If it were damnable, he being so wise,
    Why would he for the momentarie tricke
    Be perdurablie fin'de? Oh Isabell

Isa. What saies my brother?
Cla. Death is a fearefull thing

Isa. And shamed life, a hatefull

Cla. I, but to die, and go we know not where,
    To lie in cold obstruction, and to rot,
    This sensible warme motion, to become
    A kneaded clod; And the delighted spirit
    To bath in fierie floods, or to recide

William Shakespeare

In thrilling Region of thicke-ribbed Ice,
To be imprison'd in the viewlesse windes
And blowne with restlesse violence round about
The pendant world: or to be worse then worst
Of those, that lawlesse and incertaine thought,
Imagine howling, 'tis too horrible.
The weariest, and most loathed worldly life
That Age, Ache, periury, and imprisonment
Can lay on nature, is a Paradise
To what we feare of death

Isa. Alas, alas

Cla. Sweet Sister, let me liue.
What sinne you do, to saue a brothers life,
Nature dispenses with the deede so farre,
That it becomes a vertue

Isa. Oh you beast,
Oh faithlesse Coward, oh dishonest wretch,
Wilt thou be made a man, out of my vice?
Is't not a kinde of Incest, to take life
From thine owne sisters shame? What should I thinke,
Heauen shield my Mother plaid my Father faire:
For such a warped slip of wildernesse
Nere issu'd from his blood. Take my defiance,
Die, perish: Might but my bending downe
Repreeue thee from thy fate, it should proceede.
Ile pray a thousand praiers for thy death,
No word to saue thee

Cla. Nay heare me Isabell

Isa. Oh fie, fie, fie:
Thy sinn's not accidentall, but a Trade;
Mercy to thee would proue it selfe a Bawd,
'Tis best that thou diest quickly

Cla. Oh heare me Isabella

Duk. Vouchsafe a word, yong sister, but one word

Isa. What is your Will

Duk. Might you dispense with your leysure, I would by and by haue some speech with you: the satisfaction I would require, is likewise your owne benefit

Isa. I haue no superfluous leysure, my stay must be stolen out of other affaires: but I will attend you a while

Duke. Son, I haue ouer-heard what hath past between you & your sister. Angelo had neuer the purpose to corrupt her; onely he hath made an assay of her vertue, to practise his iudgement with the disposition of natures. She (hauing the truth of honour in her) hath made him that gracious deniall, which he is most glad to receiue: I am Confessor to Angelo, and I know this to be true, therfore prepare your selfe to death: do not satisfie your resolution with hopes that are fallible, to morrow you must die, goe to your knees, and make ready

Cla. Let me ask my sister pardon, I am so out of loue with life, that I will sue to be rid of it

Duke. Hold you there: farewell: Prouost, a word with you

Pro. What's your will (father?)
Duk. That now you are come, you wil be gone: leaue me a while with the Maid, my minde promises with my habit, no losse shall touch her by my company

Pro. In good time.

Enter.

Duk. The hand that hath made you faire, hath made you good: the goodnes that is cheape in beauty, makes beauty briefe in goodnes; but grace being the soule of your complexion, shall keepe the body of it euer faire: the assault that Angelo hath made to you, Fortune hath conuaid to my vnderstanding; and but that frailty hath examples for his falling, I should wonder at Angelo: how will you doe to content this Substitute, and to saue your Brother?

Isab. I am now going to resolue him: I had rather my brother die by the Law, then my sonne should be vnlawfullie borne. But (oh) how much is the good Duke deceiu'd in Angelo: if euer he returne, and I can speake to him, I will open my lips in vaine, or discouer his gouernment

Duke. That shall not be much amisse: yet, as the matter now stands, he will auoid your accusation: he made triall of you onelie. Therefore fasten your eare on my aduisings, to the loue I haue in doing good; a remedie presents it selfe. I doe make my selfe beleeue that you may most vprighteously do a poor wronged Lady a merited benefit; redeem your brother from the angry Law; doe no staine to your owne gracious person, and much please the absent Duke, if peraduenture he shall euer returne to haue hearing of this businesse

Isab. Let me heare you speake farther; I haue spirit to do any thing that appeares not fowle in the truth of my spirit

Duke. Vertue is bold, and goodnes neuer fearefull: Haue you not heard speake of Mariana the sister of Fredericke the great Souldier, who miscarried at Sea?

Isa. I haue heard of the Lady, and good words went with her name

Duke. Shee should this Angelo haue married: was affianced to her oath, and the nuptiall appointed: between which time of the contract, and limit of the solemnitie, her brother Fredericke was wrackt at Sea, hauing in that perished vessell, the dowry of his sister: but marke how heauily this befell to the poore Gentlewoman, there she lost a noble and renowned brother, in his loue toward her, euer most kinde and naturall: with him the portion and sinew of her fortune, her marriage dowry: with both, her combynate-husband, this well-seeming Angelo

Isab. Can this be so? did Angelo so leaue her? Duke. Left her in her teares, & dried not one of them with his comfort: swallowed his vowes whole, pretending in her, discoueries of dishonor: in few, bestow'd her on her owne lamentation, which she yet weares for his sake: and he, a marble to her teares, is washed with them, but relents not

Isab. What a merit were it in death to take this poore maid from the world? what corruption in this life, that it will let this man liue? But how out of this can shee auaile?
Duke. It is a rupture that you may easily heale: and the cure of it not onely saues your brother, but keepes you from dishonor in doing it

Isab. Shew me how (good Father.)
Duk. This fore-named Maid hath yet in her the continuance of her first affection: his vniust vnkindenesse (that in all reason should haue quenched her loue) hath (like an impediment in the Current) made it more violent and vnruly: Goe you to Angelo, answere his requiring with a plausible obedience, agree with his demands to the point: onely referre your selfe to this aduantage; first, that your stay with him may not be long: that the time may haue all shadow, and silence in it: and the place answere to conuenience: this being granted in course, and now followes all: wee shall aduise this wronged maid to steed vp your appointment, goe in your place: if the encounter acknowledge it selfe heereafter, it may compell him to her recompence; and heere, by this is your brother saued, your honor vntainted, the poore Mariana aduantaged, and the corrupt Deputy scaled. The Maid will I frame, and make fit for his attempt: if you thinke well to carry this as you may, the doublenes of the benefit defends the deceit from reproofe. What thinke you of it?
Isab. The image of it giues me content already, and I trust it will grow to a most prosperous perfection

Duk. It lies much in your holding vp: haste you speedily to Angelo, if for this night he intreat you to his bed, giue him promise of satisfaction:

I will presently to S[aint]. Lukes, there at the moated-Grange recides this deiected Mariana; at that place call vpon me, and dispatch with Angelo, that it may be quickly

Isab. I thank you for this comfort: fare you well good father.

Enter.

Enter Elbow, Clowne, Officers.

Elb. Nay, if there be no remedy for it, but that you will needes buy and sell men and women like beasts, we shall haue all the world drinke browne & white bastard

Duk. Oh heauens, what stuffe is heere

Clow. Twas neuer merry world since of two vsuries the merriest was put downe, and the worser allow'd by order of Law; a fur'd gowne to keepe him warme; and furd with Foxe and Lamb-skins too, to signi-fie, that craft being richer then Innocency, stands for the facing

Elb. Come your way sir: 'blesse you good Father Frier

Duk. And you good Brother Father; what offence hath this man made you, Sir?
Elb. Marry Sir, he hath offended the Law; and Sir, we take him to be a Theefe too Sir: for wee haue found vpon him Sir, a strange Pick-lock, which we haue sent to the Deputie

Duke. Fie, sirrah, a Bawd, a wicked bawd,
  The euill that thou causest to be done,
  That is thy meanes to liue. Do thou but thinke
  What 'tis to cram a maw, or cloath a backe
  From such a filthie vice: say to thy selfe,
  From their abhominable and beastly touches
  I drinke, I eate away my selfe, and liue:
  Canst thou beleeue thy liuing is a life,
  So stinkingly depending? Go mend, go mend

Clo. Indeed, it do's stinke in some sort, Sir:
　But yet Sir I would proue

Duke. Nay, if the diuell haue giuen thee proofs for sin
　　Thou wilt proue his. Take him to prison Officer:
　　Correction, and Instruction must both worke
　　Ere this rude beast will profit

Elb. He must before the Deputy Sir, he ha's giuen him warning: the Deputy cannot abide a Whore-master: if he be a Whore-monger, and comes before him, he were as good go a mile on his errand

Duke. That we were all, as some would seeme to bee
　　From our faults, as faults from seeming free.

Enter Lucio.

Elb. His necke will come to your wast, a Cord sir

Clo. I spy comfort, I cry baile: Here's a Gentleman, and a friend of mine

Luc. How now noble Pompey? What, at the wheels of Cæsar? Art thou led in triumph? What is there none of Pigmalions Images newly made woman to bee had now, for putting the hand in the pocket, and extracting clutch'd? What reply? Ha? What saist thou to this Tune, Matter, and Method? Is't not drown'd i'th last raine? Ha? What saist thou Trot? Is the world as it was Man? Which is the way? Is it sad, and few words? Or how? The tricke of it?
Duke. Still thus, and thus: still worse?
Luc. How doth my deere Morsell, thy Mistris? Procures she still? Ha?
Clo. Troth sir, shee hath eaten vp all her beefe, and she is her selfe in the tub

Luc. Why 'tis good: It is the right of it: it must be so. Euer your fresh Whore, and your pouder'd Baud, an vnshun'd consequence, it must be so. Art going to prison Pompey?

Clo. Yes faith sir

Luc. Why 'tis not amisse Pompey: farewell: goe say
    I sent thee thether: for debt Pompey? Or how?
Elb. For being a baud, for being a baud

Luc. Well, then imprison him: If imprisonment be the due of a baud, why
    'tis his right. Baud is he doubtlesse, and of antiquity too: Baud borne.
    Farwell good Pompey: Commend me to the prison Pompey, you will
    turne good husband now Pompey, you will keepe the house

Clo. I hope Sir, your good Worship wil be my baile?
Luc. No indeed wil I not Pompey, it is not the wear: I will pray (Pompey)
    to encrease your bondage if you take it not patiently: Why, your met-
    tle is the more: Adieu trustie Pompey.
Blesse you Friar

Duke. And you

Luc. Do's Bridget paint still, Pompey? Ha?
Elb. Come your waies sir, come

Clo. You will not baile me then Sir?
Luc. Then Pompey, nor now: what newes abroad Frier?
    What newes?
Elb. Come your waies sir, come

Luc. Goe to kennell (Pompey) goe:
    What newes Frier of the Duke?
Duke. I know none: can you tell me of any?
Luc. Some say he is with the Emperor of Russia: other some, he is in
    Rome: but where is he thinke you?
Duke. I know not where: but wheresoeuer, I wish him well

Luc. It was a mad fantasticall tricke of him to steale from the State, and
    vsurpe the beggerie hee was neuer borne to: Lord Angelo Dukes it
    well in his absence: he puts transgression too't

Duke. He do's well in't

Luc. A little more lenitie to Lecherie would doe no harme in him: Something too crabbed that way, Frier

Duk. It is too general a vice, and seueritie must cure it

Luc. Yes in good sooth, the vice is of a great kindred; it is well allied, but it is impossible to extirpe it quite, Frier, till eating and drinking be put downe. They say this Angelo was not made by Man and Woman, after this downe-right way of Creation: is it true, thinke you?
Duke. How should he be made then?
Luc. Some report, a Sea-maid spawn'd him. Some, that he was begot betweene two Stock-fishes. But it is certaine, that when he makes water, his Vrine is congeal'd ice, that I know to bee true: and he is a motion generatiue, that's infallible

Duke. You are pleasant sir, and speake apace

Luc. Why, what a ruthlesse thing is this in him, for the rebellion of a Cod-peece, to take away the life of a man? Would the Duke that is absent haue done this? Ere he would haue hang'd a man for the getting a hundred Bastards, he would haue paide for the Nursing a thousand. He had some feeling of the sport, hee knew the seruice, and that instructed him to mercie

Duke. I neuer heard the absent Duke much detected for Women, he was not enclin'd that way

Luc. Oh Sir, you are deceiu'd

Duke. 'Tis not possible

Luc. Who, not the Duke? Yes, your beggar of fifty: and his vse was, to put a ducket in her Clack-dish; the Duke had Crochets in him. Hee would be drunke too, that let me informe you

Duke. You do him wrong, surely

Luc. Sir, I was an inward of his: a shie fellow was the Duke, and I beleeue I know the cause of his withdrawing

Duke. What (I prethee) might be the cause?
Luc. No, pardon: 'Tis a secret must bee lockt within the teeth and the lippes: but this I can let you vnderstand, the greater file of the subiect held the Duke to be wise

Duke. Wise? Why no question but he was

Luc. A very superficiall, ignorant, vnweighing fellow
Duke. Either this is Enuie in you, Folly, or mistaking: The very streame of his life, and the businesse he hath helmed, must vppon a warranted neede, giue him a better proclamation. Let him be but testimonied in his owne bringings forth, and hee shall appeare to the enuious, a Scholler, a Statesman, and a Soldier: therefore you speake vnskilfully: or, if your knowledge bee more, it is much darkned in your malice

Luc. Sir, I know him, and I loue him

Duke. Loue talkes with better knowledge, & knowledge with deare loue

Luc. Come Sir, I know what I know

Duke. I can hardly beleeue that, since you know not what you speake. But if euer the Duke returne (as our praiers are he may) let mee desire you to make your answer before him: if it bee honest you haue spoke, you haue courage to maintaine it; I am bound to call vppon you, and I pray you your name?
Luc. Sir my name is Lucio, wel known to the Duke

Duke. He shall know you better Sir, if I may liue to report you

Luc. I feare you not

Duke. O, you hope the Duke will returne no more: or you imagine me to vnhurtfull an opposite: but indeed I can doe you little harme: You'll for-sweare this againe?
Luc. Ile be hang'd first: Thou art deceiu'd in mee Friar. But no more of this: Canst thou tell if Claudio die to morrow, or no?
Duke. Why should he die Sir?
Luc. Why? For filling a bottle with a Tunne-dish: I would the Duke we talke of were return'd againe: this vngenitur'd Agent will vn-people the Prouince with Continencie. Sparrowes must not build in his house-eeues, because they are lecherous: The Duke yet would haue darke deeds darkelie answered, hee would neuer bring them to light: would hee were return'd. Marrie this Claudio is condemned for vntrussing. Farwell good Friar, I prethee pray for me: The Duke (I say to thee againe) would eate Mutton on Fridaies. He's now past it, yet (and I say to thee) hee would mouth with a beggar, though she smelt browne-bread and Garlicke: say that I said so: Farewell.

Enter.

Duke. No might, nor greatnesse in mortality
    Can censure scape: Back-wounding calumnie
    The whitest vertue strikes. What King so strong,
    Can tie the gall vp in the slanderous tong?
    But who comes heere?

Enter Escalus, Prouost, and Bawd.

Esc. Go, away with her to prison

Bawd. Good my Lord be good to mee, your Honor is accounted a merci-full man: good my Lord

Esc. Double, and trebble admonition, and still forfeite in the same kinde?
    This would make mercy sweare and play the Tirant

Pro. A Bawd of eleuen yeares continuance, may it please your Honor

Bawd. My Lord, this is one Lucio's information against me, Mistris Kate Keepe-downe was with childe by him in the Dukes time, he promis'd her marriage: his Childe is a yeere and a quarter olde come Philip and Iacob: I haue kept it my selfe; and see how hee goes about to abuse me

Esc. That fellow is a fellow of much License: Let him be call'd before vs, Away with her to prison: Goe too, no more words. Prouost, my Brother Angelo will not be alter'd, Claudio must die to morrow: Let him be furnish'd with Diuines, and haue all charitable preparation. If my brother wrought by my pitie, it should not be so with him

Pro. So please you, this Friar hath beene with him, and aduis'd him for th' entertainment of death

Esc. Good' euen, good Father

Duke. Blisse, and goodnesse on you

Esc. Of whence are you?
Duke. Not of this Countrie, though my chance is now
    To vse it for my time: I am a brother
    Of gracious Order, late come from the Sea,
    In speciall businesse from his Holinesse

Esc. What newes abroad i'th World?
Duke. None, but that there is so great a Feauor on goodnesse, that the dissolution of it must cure it. Noueltie is onely in request, and as it is as dangerous to be aged in any kinde of course, as it is vertuous to be constant in any vndertaking. There is scarse truth enough aliue to make Societies secure, but Securitie enough to make Fellowships accurst: Much vpon this riddle runs the wisedome of the world: This newes is old enough, yet it is euerie daies newes. I pray you Sir, of what disposition was the Duke?
Esc. One, that aboue all other strifes,
    Contended especially to know himselfe

Duke. What pleasure was he giuen to?

Esc. Rather reioycing to see another merry, then merrie at anie thing which profest to make him reioice. A Gentleman of all temperance. But leaue wee him to his euents, with a praier they may proue prosperous, & let me desire to know, how you finde Claudio prepar'd? I am made to vnderstand, that you haue lent him visitation

Duke. He professes to haue receiued no sinister measure from his Iudge, but most willingly humbles himselfe to the determination of Iustice: yet had he framed to himselfe (by the instruction of his frailty) manie deceyuing promises of life, which I (by my good leisure) haue discredited to him, and now is he resolu'd to die

Esc. You haue paid the heauens your Function, and the prisoner the verie debt of your Calling. I haue labour'd for the poore Gentleman, to the extremest shore of my modestie, but my brother-Iustice haue I found so seuere, that he hath forc'd me to tell him, hee is indeede Iustice

Duke. If his owne life, Answer the straitnesse of his proceeding, It shall become him well: wherein if he chance to faile he hath sentenc'd himselfe

Esc I am going to visit the prisoner, Fare you well

Duke. Peace be with you.
    He who the sword of Heauen will beare,
    Should be as holy, as seueare:
    Patterne in himselfe to know,
    Grace to stand, and Vertue go:
    More, nor lesse to others paying,
    Then by selfe-offences weighing.
    Shame to him, whose cruell striking,
    Kils for faults of his owne liking:
    Twice trebble shame on Angelo,
    To weede my vice, and let his grow.
    Oh, what may Man within him hide,
    Though Angel on the outward side?

How may likenesse made in crimes,
Making practise on the Times,
To draw with ydle Spiders strings
Most ponderous and substantiall things?
Craft against vice, I must applie.
With Angelo to night shall lye
His old betroathed (but despised:)
So disguise shall by th' disguised
Pay with falshood, false exacting,
And performe an olde contracting.

Exit

ACTUS QUARTUS

Scoena Prima.

Enter Mariana, and Boy singing.

Song.

Take, oh take those lips away,
that so sweetly were forsworne,
And those eyes: the breake of day
lights that doe mislead the Morne;
But my kisses bring againe, bring againe,
Seales of loue, but seal'd in vaine, seal'd in vaine.

Enter Duke.

Mar. Breake off thy song, and haste thee quick away,
    Here comes a man of comfort, whose aduice
    Hath often still'd my brawling discontent.
    I cry you mercie, Sir, and well could wish
    You had not found me here so musicall.

> Let me excuse me, and beleeue me so,
> My mirth it much displeas'd, but pleas'd my woe

Duk. 'Tis good; though Musick oft hath such a charme To make bad, good; and good prouoake to harme. I pray you tell me, hath any body enquir'd for mee here to day; much vpon this time haue I promis'd here to meete

Mar. You haue not bin enquir'd after: I haue sat here all day.

Enter Isabell.

Duk. I doe constantly beleeue you: the time is come euen now. I shall craue your forbearance a little, may be I will call vpon you anone for some aduantage to your selfe

Mar. I am alwayes bound to you.

Enter.

Duk. Very well met, and well come:
  What is the newes from this good Deputie?
Isab. He hath a Garden circummur'd with Bricke,
  Whose westerne side is with a Vineyard back't;
  And to that Vineyard is a planched gate,
  That makes his opening with this bigger Key:
  This other doth command a little doore,
  Which from the Vineyard to the Garden leades,
  There haue I made my promise, vpon the
  Heauy midle of the night, to call vpon him

Duk. But shall you on your knowledge find this **way**?
Isab. I haue t'ane a due, and wary note vpon't,
  With whispering, and most guiltie diligence,
  In action all of precept, he did show me
  The way twice ore

Duk. Are there no other tokens
    Betweene you 'greed, concerning her obseruance?
Isab. No: none but onely a repaire ith' darke,
    And that I haue possest him, my most stay
    Can be but briefe: for I haue made him know,
    I haue a Seruant comes with me along
    That staies vpon me; whose perswasion is,
    I come about my Brother

Duk. 'Tis well borne vp.
    I haue not yet made knowne to Mariana

Enter Mariana.

A word of this: what hoa, within; come forth,
I pray you be acquainted with this Maid,
She comes to doe you good

Isab. I doe desire the like

Duk. Do you perswade your selfe that I respect you?
Mar. Good Frier, I know you do, and haue found it

Duke. Take then this your companion by the hand
    Who hath a storie readie for your eare:
    I shall attend your leisure, but make haste
    The vaporous night approaches

Mar. Wilt please you walke aside.

Enter.

Duke. Oh Place, and greatnes: millions of false eies
    Are stucke vpon thee: volumes of report
    Run with these false, and most contrarious Quest
    Vpon thy doings: thousand escapes of wit
    Make thee the father of their idle dreame,
    And racke thee in their fancies. Welcome, how agreed?

Enter Mariana and Isabella.

Isab. Shee'll take the enterprize vpon her father,
   If you aduise it

Duke. It is not my consent,
   But my entreaty too

Isa. Little haue you to say
   When you depart from him, but soft and low,
   Remember now my brother

Mar. Feare me not

Duk. Nor gentle daughter, feare you not at all:
   He is your husband on a pre-contract:
   To bring you thus together 'tis no sinne,
   Sith that the Iustice of your title to him
   Doth flourish the deceit. Come, let vs goe,
   Our Corne's to reape, for yet our Tithes to sow.

Exeunt.

Scena Secunda.

Enter Prouost and Clowne.

Pro. Come hither sirha; can you cut off a mans head?
Clo. If the man be a Bachelor Sir, I can:
   But if he be a married man, he's his wiues head,
   And I can neuer cut off a womans head

Pro. Come sir, leaue me your snatches, and yeeld mee a direct answere. To
   morrow morning are to die Claudio and Barnardine: heere is in our
   prison a common executioner, who in his office lacks a helper, if you

will take it on you to assist him, it shall redeeme you from your Gyues: if not, you shall haue your full time of imprisonment, and your deliuerance with an vnpittied whipping; for you haue beene a notorious bawd

Clo. Sir, I haue beene an vnlawfull bawd, time out of minde, but yet I will bee content to be a lawfull hangman: I would bee glad to receiue some instruction from my fellow partner

Pro. What hoa, Abhorson: where's Abhorson there?

Enter Abhorson.

Abh. Doe you call sir?
Pro. Sirha, here's a fellow will helpe you to morrow in your execution: if you thinke it meet, compound with him by the yeere, and let him abide here with you, if not, vse him for the present, and dismisse him, hee cannot plead his estimation with you: he hath beene a Bawd

Abh. A Bawd Sir? fie vpon him, he will discredit our mysterie

Pro. Goe too Sir, you waigh equallie: a feather will turne the Scale.

Enter.

Clo. Pray sir, by your good fauor: for surely sir, a good fauor you haue, but that you haue a hanging look: Doe you call sir, your occupation a Mysterie?
Abh. I Sir, a Misterie

Clo. Painting Sir, I haue heard say, is a Misterie; and your Whores sir, being members of my occupation, vsing painting, do proue my Occupation, a Misterie: but what Misterie there should be in hanging, if I should be hang'd, I cannot imagine

Abh. Sir, it is a Misterie

Clo. Proofe

Abh. Euerie true mans apparrell fits your Theefe

Clo. If it be too little for your theefe, your true man thinkes it bigge enough. If it bee too bigge for your Theefe, your Theefe thinkes it little enough: So euerie true mans apparrell fits your Theefe.
Enter Prouost.

Pro. Are you agreed?
Clo. Sir, I will serue him: For I do finde your Hangman is a more penitent Trade then your Bawd: he doth oftner aske forgiuenesse

Pro. You sirrah, prouide your blocke and your Axe to morrow, foure a clocke

Abh. Come on (Bawd) I will instruct thee in my
    Trade: follow

Clo. I do desire to learne sir: and I hope, if you haue occasion to vse me for your owne turne, you shall finde me y'are. For truly sir, for your kindnesse, I owe you a good turne.

Exit

Pro. Call hether Barnardine and Claudio:
    Th' one has my pitie; not a iot the other,
    Being a Murtherer, though he were my brother.

Enter Claudio.

Looke, here's the Warrant Claudio, for thy death,
'Tis now dead midnight, and by eight to morrow
Thou must be made immortall. Where's Barnardine?
Cla. As fast lock'd vp in sleepe, as guiltlesse labour,
When it lies starkely in the Trauellers bones,
He will not wake

Pro. Who can do good on him?
    Well, go, prepare your selfe. But harke, what noise?
    Heauen giue your spirits comfort: by, and by,
    I hope it is some pardon, or repreeue
    For the most gentle Claudio. Welcome Father.

Enter Duke.

Duke. The best, and wholsomst spirits of the night,
    Inuellop you, good Prouost: who call'd heere of late?
Pro. None since the Curphew rung

Duke. Not Isabell?
Pro. No

Duke. They will then er't be long

Pro. What comfort is for Claudio?
Duke. There's some in hope

Pro. It is a bitter Deputie

Duke. Not so, not so: his life is paralel'd
    Euen with the stroke and line of his great Iustice:
    He doth with holie abstinence subdue
    That in himselfe, which he spurres on his powre
    To qualifie in others: were he meal'd with that
    Which he corrects, then were he tirrannous,
    But this being so, he's iust. Now are they come.
    This is a gentle Prouost, sildome when
    The steeled Gaoler is the friend of men:
    How now? what noise? That spirit's possest with hast,
    That wounds th' vnsisting Posterne with these strokes

Pro. There he must stay vntil the Officer
    Arise to let him in: he is call'd vp

Duke. Haue you no countermand for Claudio yet?
    But he must die to morrow?
Pro. None Sir, none

Duke. As neere the dawning Prouost, as it is,
    You shall heare more ere Morning

Pro. Happely
    You something know: yet I beleeue there comes
    No countermand: no such example haue we:
    Besides, vpon the verie siege of Iustice,
    Lord Angelo hath to the publike eare
    Profest the contrarie.

Enter a Messenger.

Duke. This is his Lords man

Pro. And heere comes Claudio's pardon

Mess. My Lord hath sent you this note,
    And by mee this further charge;
    That you swerue not from the smallest Article of it,
    Neither in time, matter, or other circumstance.
    Good morrow: for as I take it, it is almost day

Pro. I shall obey him

Duke. This is his Pardon purchas'd by such sin,
    For which the Pardoner himselfe is in:
    Hence hath offence his quicke celeritie,
    When it is borne in high Authority.
    When Vice makes Mercie; Mercie's so extended,
    That for the faults loue, is th' offender friended.
    Now Sir, what newes?

Pro. I told you:
   Lord Angelo (be-like) thinking me remisse
   In mine Office, awakens mee
   With this vnwonted putting on, methinks strangely:
   For he hath not vs'd it before

Duk. Pray you let's heare.

The Letter.

Whatsoeuer you may heare to the contrary, let Claudio be executed by foure of the clocke, and in the afternoone Bernardine: For my better satisfaction, let mee haue Claudios head sent me by fiue. Let this be duely performed with a thought that more depends on it, then we must yet deliuer. Thus faile not to doe your Office, as you will answere it at your perill. What say you to this Sir?
Duke. What is that Barnardine, who is to be executed in th' afternoone?
Pro. A Bohemian borne: But here nurst vp & bred,
   One that is a prisoner nine yeeres old

Duke. How came it, that the absent Duke had not either deliuer'd him to
   his libertie, or executed him? I haue heard it was euer his manner to
   do so

Pro. His friends still wrought Repreeues for him:
   And indeed his fact till now in the gouernment of Lord
   Angelo, came not to an vndoubtfull proofe

Duke. It is now apparant?
Pro. Most manifest, and not denied by himselfe

Duke. Hath he borne himselfe penitently in prison?
   How seemes he to be touch'd?
Pro. A man that apprehends death no more dreadfully, but as a drunken
   sleepe, carelesse, wreaklesse, and fearelesse of what's past, present, or
   to come: insensible of mortality, and desperately mortall

Duke. He wants aduice

Pro. He wil heare none: he hath euermore had the liberty of the prison: giue him leaue to escape hence, hee would not. Drunke many times a day, if not many daies entirely drunke. We haue verie oft awak'd him, as if to carrie him to execution, and shew'd him a seeming warrant for it, it hath not moued him at all

Duke. More of him anon: There is written in your brow Prouost, honesty and constancie; if I reade it not truly, my ancient skill beguiles me: but in the boldnes of my cunning, I will lay my selfe in hazard: Claudio, whom heere you haue warrant to execute, is no greater forfeit to the Law, then Angelo who hath sentenc'd him. To make you vnderstand this in a manifested effect, I craue but foure daies respit: for the which, you are to do me both a present, and a dangerous courtesie

Pro. Pray Sir, in what?
Duke. In the delaying death

Pro. Alacke, how may I do it? Hauing the houre limited, and an expresse command, vnder penaltie, to deliuer his head in the view of Angelo? I may make my case as Claudio's, to crosse this in the smallest

Duke. By the vow of mine Order, I warrant you,
   If my instructions may be your guide,
   Let this Barnardine be this morning executed,
   And his head borne to Angelo

Pro. Angelo hath seene them both,
   And will discouer the fauour

Duke. Oh, death's a great disguiser, and you may adde to it; Shaue the head, and tie the beard, and say it was the desire of the penitent to be so bar'de before his death: you know the course is common. If any thing fall to you vpon this, more then thankes and good fortune, by the Saint whom I professe, I will plead against it with my life

Pro. Pardon me, good Father, it is against my oath

Duke. Were you sworne to the Duke, or to the Deputie?
Pro. To him, and to his Substitutes

Duke. You will thinke you haue made no offence, if the Duke auouch the iustice of your dealing?
Pro. But what likelihood is in that?
Duke. Not a resemblance, but a certainty; yet since I see you fearfull, that neither my coate, integrity, nor perswasion, can with ease attempt you, I wil go further then I meant, to plucke all feares out of you. Looke you Sir, heere is the hand and Seale of the Duke: you know the Charracter I doubt not, and the Signet is not strange to you?
Pro. I know them both

Duke. The Contents of this, is the returne of the Duke; you shall anon ouer-reade it at your pleasure: where you shall finde within these two daies, he wil be heere. This is a thing that Angelo knowes not, for hee this very day receiues letters of strange tenor, perchance of the Dukes death, perchance entering into some Monasterie, but by chance nothing of what is writ. Looke, th' vnfolding Starre calles vp the Shepheard; put not your selfe into amazement, how these things should be; all difficulties are but easie when they are knowne. Call your executioner, and off with Barnardines head: I will giue him a present shrift, and aduise him for a better place. Yet you are amaz'd, but this shall absolutely resolue you: Come away, it is almost cleere dawne.

Enter.

Scena Tertia.

Enter Clowne.

Clo. I am as well acquainted heere, as I was in our house of profession: one would thinke it were Mistris Ouerdons owne house, for heere be manie of her olde Customers. First, here's yong Mr Rash, hee's in for a commoditie of browne paper, and olde Ginger, nine score and seuenteene pounds, of which hee made fiue Markes readie money: marrie then, Ginger was not much in request, for the olde Women were all dead. Then is there heere one Mr Caper, at the suite of Master Three-Pile the Mercer, for some foure suites of Peachcolour'd Satten, which now peaches him a beggar. Then haue we heere, yong Dizie, and yong Mr Deepevow, and Mr Copperspurre, and Mr Starue-Lackey the Rapier and dagger man, and yong Drop-heire that kild lustie Pudding, and Mr Forthlight the Tilter, and braue Mr Shootie the great Traueller, and wilde Halfe-Canne that stabb'd Pots, and I thinke fortie more, all great doers in our Trade, and are now for the Lords sake.

Enter Abhorson.

Abh. Sirrah, bring Barnardine hether

Clo. Mr Barnardine, you must rise and be hang'd,
    Mr Barnardine

Abh. What hoa Barnardine.

Barnardine within.

Bar. A pox o'your throats: who makes that noyse there? What are you?
Clo. Your friends Sir, the Hangman:
    You must be so good Sir to rise, and be put to death

Bar. Away you Rogue, away, I am sleepie

Abh. Tell him he must awake,
    And that quickly too

Clo. Pray Master Barnardine, awake till you are executed, and sleepe afterwards

Ab. Go in to him, and fetch him out

Clo. He is comming Sir, he is comming: I heare his
    Straw russle.

Enter Barnardine.

Abh. Is the Axe vpon the blocke, sirrah?
Clo. Verie readie Sir

Bar. How now Abhorson?
    What's the newes with you?
Abh. Truly Sir, I would desire you to clap into your prayers: for looke you,
    the Warrants come

Bar. You Rogue, I haue bin drinking all night,
    I am not fitted for't

Clo. Oh, the better Sir: for he that drinkes all night, and is hanged betimes
    in the morning, may sleepe the sounder all the next day.

Enter Duke.

Abh. Looke you Sir, heere comes your ghostly Father: do we iest now
    thinke you?
Duke. Sir, induced by my charitie, and hearing how hastily you are to
    depart, I am come to aduise you, Comfort you, and pray with you

Bar. Friar, not I: I haue bin drinking hard all night, and I will haue more
    time to prepare mee, or they shall beat out my braines with billets: I
    will not consent to die this day, that's certaine

Duke. Oh sir, you must: and therefore I beseech you
    Looke forward on the iournie you shall go

Bar. I sweare I will not die to day for anie mans perswasion

Duke. But heare you:
Bar. Not a word: if you haue anie thing to say to me, come to my Ward:
for thence will not I to day.

Exit

Enter Prouost.

Duke. Vnfit to liue, or die: oh grauell heart.
After him (Fellowes) bring him to the blocke

Pro. Now Sir, how do you finde the prisoner?
Duke. A creature vnprepar'd, vnmeet for death,
And to transport him in the minde he is,
Were damnable

Pro. Heere in the prison, Father,
There died this morning of a cruell Feauor,
One Ragozine, a most notorious Pirate,
A man of Claudio's yeares: his beard, and head
Iust of his colour. What if we do omit
This Reprobate, til he were wel enclin'd,
And satisfie the Deputie with the visage
Of Ragozine, more like to Claudio?
Duke. Oh, 'tis an accident that heauen prouides:
Dispatch it presently, the houre drawes on
Prefixt by Angelo: See this be done,
And sent according to command, whiles I
Perswade this rude wretch willingly to die

Pro. This shall be done (good Father) presently:
But Barnardine must die this afternoone,
And how shall we continue Claudio,
To saue me from the danger that might come,
If he were knowne aliue?
Duke. Let this be done,
Put them in secret holds, both Barnardine and Claudio,

Ere twice the Sun hath made his iournall greeting
To yond generation, you shal finde
Your safetie manifested

Pro. I am your free dependant.

Enter.

Duke. Quicke, dispatch, and send the head to Angelo
    Now wil I write Letters to Angelo,
    (The Prouost he shal beare them) whose contents
    Shal witnesse to him I am neere at home:
    And that by great Iniunctions I am bound
    To enter publikely: him Ile desire
    To meet me at the consecrated Fount,
    A League below the Citie: and from thence,
    By cold gradation, and weale-ballanc'd forme.
    We shal proceed with Angelo.

Enter Prouost.

Pro. Heere is the head, Ile carrie it my selfe

Duke. Conuenient is it: Make a swift returne,
    For I would commune with you of such things,
    That want no eare but yours

Pro. Ile make all speede.

Exit

Isabell within.

Isa. Peace hoa, be heere

Duke. The tongue of Isabell. She's come to know,
    If yet her brothers pardon be come hither:

But I will keepe her ignorant of her good,
To make her heauenly comforts of dispaire,
When it is least expected.

Enter Isabella.

Isa. Hoa, by your leaue

Duke. Good morning to you, faire, and gracious daughter

Isa. The better giuen me by so holy a man,
    Hath yet the Deputie sent my brothers pardon?
Duke. He hath releasd him, Isabell, from the world,
    His head is off, and sent to Angelo

Isa. Nay, but it is not so

Duke. It is no other,
    Shew your wisedome daughter in your close patience

Isa. Oh, I wil to him, and plucke out his eies

Duk. You shal not be admitted to his sight

Isa. Vnhappie Claudio, wretched Isabell,
    Iniurious world, most damned Angelo

Duke. This nor hurts him, nor profits you a iot,
    Forbeare it therefore, giue your cause to heauen.
    Marke what I say, which you shal finde
    By euery sillable a faithful veritie.
    The Duke comes home to morrow: nay drie your eyes,
    One of our Couent, and his Confessor
    Giues me this instance: Already he hath carried
    Notice to Escalus and Angelo,
    Who do prepare to meete him at the gates,
    There to giue vp their powre: If you can pace your wisdom,
    In that good path that I would wish it go,

> And you shal haue your bosome on this wretch,
> Grace of the Duke, reuenges to your heart,
> And general Honor

Isa. I am directed by you

Duk. This Letter then to Friar Peter giue,
'Tis that he sent me of the Dukes returne:
Say, by this token, I desire his companie
At Mariana's house to night. Her cause, and yours
Ile perfect him withall, and he shal bring you
Before the Duke; and to the head of Angelo
Accuse him home and home. For my poore selfe,
I am combined by a sacred Vow,
And shall be absent. Wend you with this Letter:
Command these fretting waters from your eies
With a light heart; trust not my holie Order
If I peruert your course: whose heere?

Enter Lucio.

Luc. Good' euen;
   Frier, where's the Prouost?
Duke. Not within Sir

Luc. Oh prettie Isabella, I am pale at mine heart, to see thine eyes so red: thou must be patient; I am faine to dine and sup with water and bran: I dare not for my head fill my belly. One fruitful Meale would set mee too't: but they say the Duke will be heere to Morrow. By my troth Isabell I lou'd thy brother, if the olde fantastical Duke of darke corners had bene at home, he had liued

Duke. Sir, the Duke is marueilous little beholding to your reports, but the best is, he liues not in them

Luc. Friar, thou knowest not the Duke so wel as I do: he's a better woodman then thou tak'st him for

Duke. Well: you'l answer this one day. Fare ye well

Luc. Nay tarrie, Ile go along with thee,
    I can tel thee pretty tales of the Duke

Duke. You haue told me too many of him already sir if they be true: if not true, none were enough

Lucio. I was once before him for getting a Wench with childe

Duke. Did you such a thing?
Luc. Yes marrie did I; but I was faine to forswear it,
    They would else haue married me to the rotten Medler

Duke. Sir your company is fairer then honest, rest you well

Lucio. By my troth Ile go with thee to the lanes end: if baudy talke offend you, wee'l haue very litle of it: nay Friar, I am a kind of Burre, I shal sticke.

Exeunt.

Scena Quarta.

Enter Angelo & Escalus.

Esc. Euery Letter he hath writ, hath disuouch'd other

An. In most vneuen and distracted manner, his actions show much like to madnesse, pray heauen his wisedome bee not tainted: and why meet him at the gates and deliuer our authorities there?
Esc. I ghesse not

Ang. And why should wee proclaime it in an howre before his entring, that if any craue redresse of iniustice, they should exhibit their petitions in the street?

Esc. He showes his reason for that: to haue a dispatch of Complaints, and to deliuer vs from deuices heereafter, which shall then haue no power to stand against vs

Ang. Well: I beseech you let it bee proclaim'd betimes i'th' morne, Ile call you at your house: giue notice to such men of sort and suite as are to meete him

Esc. I shall sir: fareyouwell.

Enter.

Ang. Good night.
    This deede vnshapes me quite, makes me vnpregnant
    And dull to all proceedings. A deflowred maid,
    And by an eminent body, that enforc'd
    The Law against it? But that her tender shame
    Will not proclaime against her maiden losse,
    How might she tongue me? yet reason dares her no,
    For my Authority beares of a credent bulke,
    That no particular scandall once can touch
    But it confounds the breather. He should haue liu'd,
    Saue that his riotous youth with dangerous sense
    Might in the times to come haue ta'ne reuenge
    By so receiuing a dishonor'd life
    With ransome of such shame: would yet he had liued.
    Alack, when once our grace we haue forgot,
    Nothing goes right, we would, and we would not.

Enter.

Scena Quinta.

Enter Duke and Frier Peter.

Duke. These Letters at fit time deliuer me,
    The Prouost knowes our purpose and our plot,

> The matter being a foote, keepe your instruction
> And hold you euer to our speciall drift,
> Though sometimes you doe blench from this to that
> As cause doth minister: Goe call at Flauia's house,
> And tell him where I stay: giue the like notice
> To Valencius, Rowland, and to Crassus,
> And bid them bring the Trumpets to the gate:
> But send me Flauius first

Peter. It shall be speeded well.

Enter Varrius.

Duke. I thank thee Varrius, thou hast made good hast,
    Come, we will walke: There's other of our friends
    Will greet vs heere anon: my gentle Varrius.

Exeunt.

Scena Sexta.

Enter Isabella and Mariana.

Isab. To speake so indirectly I am loath,
    I would say the truth, but to accuse him so
    That is your part, yet I am aduis'd to doe it,
    He saies, to vaile full purpose

Mar. Be rul'd by him

Isab. Besides he tells me, that if peraduenture
    He speake against me on the aduerse side,
    I should not thinke it strange, for 'tis a physicke
    That's bitter, to sweet end.

Enter Peter.

Mar. I would Frier Peter
Isab. Oh peace, the Frier is come

Peter. Come I haue found you out a stand most fit,
   Where you may haue such vantage on the Duke
   He shall not passe you:
   Twice haue the Trumpets sounded.
   The generous, and grauest Citizens
   Haue hent the gates, and very neere vpon
   The Duke is entring:
   Therefore hence away.

Exeunt.

ACTUS QUINTUS

Scoena Prima.

Enter Duke, Varrius, Lords, Angelo, Esculus, Lucio, Citizens at seuerall doores.

Duk. My very worthy Cosen, fairely met,
    Our old, and faithfull friend, we are glad to see you

Ang. Esc. Happy returne be to your royall grace

Duk. Many and harty thankings to you both:
    We haue made enquiry of you, and we heare
    Such goodnesse of your Iustice, that our soule
    Cannot but yeeld you forth to publique thankes
    Forerunning more requitall

Ang. You make my bonds still greater

Duk. Oh your desert speaks loud, & I should wrong it
    To locke it in the wards of couert bosome

When it deserues with characters of brasse
A forted residence 'gainst the tooth of time,
And razure of obliuion: Giue we your hand
And let the Subiect see, to make them know
That outward curtesies would faine proclaime
Fauours that keepe within: Come Escalus,
You must walke by vs, on our other hand:
And good supporters are you.

Enter Peter and Isabella.

Peter. Now is your time
Speake loud, and kneele before him

Isab. Iustice, O royall Duke, vaile your regard
Vpon a wrong'd (I would faine haue said a Maid)
Oh worthy Prince, dishonor not your eye
By throwing it on any other obiect,
Till you haue heard me, in my true complaint,
And giuen me Iustice, Iustice, Iustice, Iustice

Duk. Relate your wrongs;
In what, by whom? be briefe:
Here is Lord Angelo shall giue you Iustice,
Reueale your selfe to him

Isab. Oh worthy Duke,
You bid me seeke redemption of the diuell,
Heare me your selfe: for that which I must speake
Must either punish me, not being beleeu'd,
Or wring redresse from you:
Heare me: oh heare me, heere

Ang. My Lord, her wits I feare me are not firme:
She hath bin a suitor to me, for her Brother
Cut off by course of Iustice

Isab. By course of Iustice

Ang. And she will speake most bitterly, and strange

Isab. Most strange: but yet most truely wil I speake,
    That Angelo's forsworne, is it not strange?
    That Angelo's a murtherer, is't not strange?
    That Angelo is an adulterous thiefe,
    An hypocrite, a virgin violator,
    Is it not strange? and strange?
Duke. Nay it is ten times strange?
Isa. It is not truer he is Angelo,
    Then this is all as true, as it is strange;
    Nay, it is ten times true, for truth is truth
    To th' end of reckning

Duke. Away with her: poore soule
    She speakes this, in th' infirmity of sence

Isa. Oh Prince, I coniure thee, as thou beleeu'st
    There is another comfort, then this world,
    That thou neglect me not, with that opinion
    That I am touch'd with madnesse: make not impossible
    That which but seemes vnlike, 'tis not impossible
    But one, the wickedst caitiffe on the ground
    May seeme as shie, as graue, as iust, as absolute:
    As Angelo, euen so may Angelo
    In all his dressings, caracts, titles, formes,
    Be an arch-villaine: Beleeue it, royall Prince
    If he be lesse, he's nothing, but he's more,
    Had I more name for badnesse

Duke. By mine honesty
    If she be mad, as I beleeue no other,
    Her madnesse hath the oddest frame of sense,
    Such a dependancy of thing, on thing,
    As ere I heard in madnesse

Isab. Oh gracious Duke
   Harpe not on that; nor do not banish reason
   For inequality, but let your reason serue
   To make the truth appeare, where it seemes hid,
   And hide the false seemes true

Duk. Many that are not mad
   Haue sure more lacke of reason:
   What would you say?
Isab. I am the Sister of one Claudio,
   Condemnd vpon the Act of Fornication
   To loose his head, condemn'd by Angelo,
   I, (in probation of a Sisterhood)
   Was sent to by my Brother; one Lucio
   As then the Messenger

Luc. That's I, and't like your Grace:
   I came to her from Claudio, and desir'd her,
   To try her gracious fortune with Lord Angelo,
   For her poore Brothers pardon

Isab. That's he indeede

Duk. You were not bid to speake

Luc. No, my good Lord,
   Nor wish'd to hold my peace

Duk. I wish you now then,
   Pray you take note of it: and when you haue
   A businesse for your selfe: pray heauen you then
   Be perfect

Luc. I warrant your honor

Duk. The warrant's for your selfe: take heede to't

Isab. This Gentleman told somewhat of my Tale

Luc. Right

Duk. It may be right, but you are i'the wrong
    To speake before your time: proceed,
Isab. I went
    To this pernicious Caitiffe Deputie

Duk. That's somewhat madly spoken

Isab. Pardon it,
    The phrase is to the matter

Duke. Mended againe: the matter: proceed

Isab. In briefe, to set the needlesse processe by:
    How I perswaded, how I praid, and kneel'd,
    How he refeld me, and how I replide
    (For this was of much length) the vild conclusion
    I now begin with griefe, and shame to vtter.
    He would not, but by gift of my chaste body
    To his concupiscible intemperate lust
    Release my brother; and after much debatement,
    My sisterly remorse, confutes mine honour,
    And I did yeeld to him: But the next morne betimes,
    His purpose surfetting, he sends a warrant
    For my poore brothers head

Duke. This is most likely

Isab. Oh that it were as like as it is true

Duk. By heauen (fond wretch) y knowst not what thou speak'st,
    Or else thou art suborn'd against his honor
    In hatefull practise: first his Integritie

Stands without blemish: next it imports no reason,
That with such vehemency he should pursue
Faults proper to himselfe: if he had so offended
He would haue waigh'd thy brother by himselfe,
And not haue cut him off: some one hath set you on:
Confesse the truth, and say by whose aduice
Thou cam'st heere to complaine

Isab. And is this all?
Then oh you blessed Ministers aboue
Keepe me in patience, and with ripened time
Vnfold the euill, which is heere wrapt vp
In countenance: heauen shield your Grace from woe,
As I thus wrong'd, hence vnbeleeued goe

Duke. I know you'ld faine be gone: An Officer:
To prison with her: Shall we thus permit
A blasting and a scandalous breath to fall,
On him so neere vs? This needs must be a practise:
Who knew of your intent and comming hither?
Isa. One that I would were heere, Frier Lodowick

Duk. A ghostly Father, belike:
Who knowes that Lodowicke?
Luc. My Lord, I know him, 'tis a medling Fryer,
I doe not like the man: had he been Lay my Lord,
For certaine words he spake against your Grace
In your retirment, I had swing'd him soundly

Duke. Words against mee? this' a good Fryer belike
And to set on this wretched woman here
Against our Substitute: Let this Fryer be found

Luc. But yesternight my Lord, she and that Fryer
I saw them at the prison: a sawcy Fryar,
A very scuruy fellow

Peter. Blessed be your Royall Grace:
    I haue stood by my Lord, and I haue heard
    Your royall eare abus'd: first hath this woman
    Most wrongfully accus'd your Substitute,
    Who is as free from touch, or soyle with her
    As she from one vngot

Duke. We did beleeue no lesse.
    Know you that Frier Lodowick that she speakes of?
Peter. I know him for a man diuine and holy,
    Not scuruy, nor a temporary medler
    As he's reported by this Gentleman:
    And on my trust, a man that neuer yet
    Did (as he vouches) mis-report your Grace

Luc. My Lord, most villanously, beleeue it

Peter. Well: he in time may come to cleere himselfe;
    But at this instant he is sicke, my Lord:
    Of a strange Feauor: vpon his meere request
    Being come to knowledge, that there was complaint
    Intended 'gainst Lord Angelo, came I hether
    To speake as from his mouth, what he doth know
    Is true, and false: And what he with his oath
    And all probation will make vp full cleare
    Whensoeuer he's conuented: First for this woman,
    To iustifie this worthy Noble man
    So vulgarly and personally accus'd,
    Her shall you heare disproued to her eyes,
    Till she her selfe confesse it

Duk. Good Frier, let's heare it:
    Doe you not smile at this, Lord Angelo?
    Oh heauen, the vanity of wretched fooles.
    Giue vs some seates, Come cosen Angelo,
    In this I'll be impartiall: be you Iudge
    Of your owne Cause: Is this the Witnes Frier?

Enter Mariana.

First, let her shew your face, and after, speake

Mar. Pardon my Lord, I will not shew my face
    Vntill my husband bid me

Duke. What, are you married?
Mar. No my Lord

Duke. Are you a Maid?
Mar. No my Lord

Duk. A Widow then?
Mar. Neither, my Lord

Duk. Why you are nothing then: neither Maid, Widow, nor Wife?
Luc. My Lord, she may be a Puncke: for many of them, are neither Maid,
    Widow, nor Wife

Duk. Silence that fellow: I would he had some cause to prattle for himselfe

Luc. Well my Lord

Mar. My Lord, I doe confesse I nere was married,
    And I confesse besides, I am no Maid,
    I haue known my husband, yet my husband
    Knowes not, that euer he knew me

Luc. He was drunk then, my Lord, it can be no better

Duk. For the benefit of silence, would thou wert so to

Luc. Well, my Lord

Duk. This is no witnesse for Lord Angelo

Mar. Now I come to't, my Lord.
    Shee that accuses him of Fornication,
    In selfe-same manner, doth accuse my husband,
    And charges him, my Lord, with such a time,
    When I'le depose I had him in mine Armes
    With all th' effect of Loue

Ang. Charges she moe then me?
Mar. Not that I know

Duk. No? you say your husband

Mar. Why iust, my Lord, and that is Angelo,
    Who thinkes he knowes, that he nere knew my body,
    But knowes, he thinkes, that he knowes Isabels

Ang. This is a strange abuse: Let's see thy face

Mar. My husband bids me, now I will vnmaske.
    This is that face, thou cruell Angelo
    Which once thou sworst, was worth the looking on:
    This is the hand, which with a vowd contract
    Was fast belockt in thine: This is the body
    That tooke away the match from Isabell,
    And did supply thee at thy garden-house
    In her Imagin'd person

Duke. Know you this woman?
Luc. Carnallie she saies

Duk. Sirha, no more

Luc. Enough my Lord

Ang. My Lord, I must confesse, I know this woman,
    And fiue yeres since there was some speech of marriage
    Betwixt my selfe, and her: which was broke off,

     Partly for that her promis'd proportions
     Came short of Composition: But in chiefe
     For that her reputation was dis-valued
     In leuitie: Since which time of fiue yeres
     I neuer spake with her, saw her, nor heard from her
     Vpon my faith, and honor

Mar. Noble Prince,
     As there comes light from heauen, and words fro[m] breath,
     As there is sence in truth, and truth in vertue,
     I am affianced this mans wife, as strongly
     As words could make vp vowes: And my good Lord,
     But Tuesday night last gon, in's garden house,
     He knew me as a wife. As this is true,
     Let me in safety raise me from my knees,
     Or else for euer be confixed here
     A Marble Monument

Ang. I did but smile till now,
     Now, good my Lord, giue me the scope of Iustice,
     My patience here is touch'd: I doe perceiue
     These poore informall women, are no more
     But instruments of some more mightier member
     That sets them on. Let me haue way, my Lord
     To finde this practise out

Duke. I, with my heart,
     And punish them to your height of pleasure.
     Thou foolish Frier, and thou pernicious woman
     Compact with her that's gone: thinkst thou, thy oathes,
     Though they would swear downe each particular Saint,
     Were testimonies against his worth, and credit
     That's seal'd in approbation? you, Lord Escalus
     Sit with my Cozen, lend him your kinde paines
     To finde out this abuse, whence 'tis deriu'd.
     There is another Frier that set them on,
     Let him be sent for

Peter. Would he were here, my Lord, for he indeed
    Hath set the women on to this Complaint;
    Your Prouost knowes the place where he abides,
    And he may fetch him

Duke. Goe, doe it instantly:
    And you, my noble and well-warranted Cosen
    Whom it concernes to heare this matter forth,
    Doe with your iniuries as seemes you best
    In any chastisement; I for a while
    Will leaue you; but stir not you till you haue
    Well determin'd vpon these Slanderers.

Enter.

Esc. My Lord, wee'll doe it throughly: Signior Lucio, did not you say you knew that Frier Lodowick to be a dishonest person?
Luc. Cucullus non facit Monachum, honest in nothing but in his Clothes, and one that hath spoke most villainous speeches of the Duke

Esc. We shall intreat you to abide heere till he come, and inforce them against him: we shall finde this Frier a notable fellow

Luc. As any in Vienna, on my word

Esc. Call that same Isabell here once againe, I would speake with her: pray you, my Lord, giue mee leaue to question, you shall see how Ile handle her

Luc. Not better then he, by her owne report

Esc. Say you?
Luc. Marry sir, I thinke, if you handled her priuately She would sooner confesse, perchance publikely she'll be asham'd.

Enter Duke, Prouost, Isabella

Esc. I will goe darkely to worke with her

Luc. That's the way: for women are light at midnight

Esc. Come on Mistris, here's a Gentlewoman,
   Denies all that you haue said

Luc. My Lord, here comes the rascall I spoke of,
   Here, with the Prouost

Esc. In very good time: speake not you to him, till we call vpon you

Luc. Mum

Esc. Come Sir, did you set these women on to slander
   Lord Angelo? they haue confes'd you did

Duk. 'Tis false

Esc. How? Know you where you are?
Duk. Respect to your great place; and let the diuell
   Be sometime honour'd, for his burning throne.
   Where is the Duke? 'tis he should heare me speake

Esc. The Duke's in vs: and we will heare you speake,
   Looke you speake iustly

Duk. Boldly, at least. But oh poore soules,
   Come you to seeke the Lamb here of the Fox;
   Good night to your redresse: Is the Duke gone?
   Then is your cause gone too: The Duke's vniust,
   Thus to retort your manifest Appeale,
   And put your triall in the villaines mouth,
   Which here you come to accuse

Luc. This is the rascall: this is he I spoke of

Esc. Why thou vnreuerend, and vnhallowed Fryer:
   Is't not enough thou hast suborn'd these women,
      To accuse this worthy man? but in foule mouth,
      And in the witnesse of his proper eare,
      To call him villaine; and then to glance from him,
      To th'Duke himselfe, to taxe him with Iniustice?
      Take him hence; to th' racke with him: we'll towze you
      Ioynt by ioynt, but we will know his purpose:
      What? vniust?
Duk. Be not so hot: the Duke dare
      No more stretch this finger of mine, then he
      Dare racke his owne: his Subiect am I not,
      Nor here Prouinciall: My businesse in this State
      Made me a looker on here in Vienna,
      Where I haue seene corruption boyle and bubble,
      Till it ore-run the Stew: Lawes, for all faults,
      But faults so countenanc'd, that the strong Statutes
      Stand like the forfeites in a Barbers shop,
      As much in mocke, as marke

Esc. Slander to th' State:
      Away with him to prison

Ang. What can you vouch against him Signior Lucio?
      Is this the man you did tell vs of?
Luc. 'Tis he, my Lord: come hither goodman bald-pate, doe you know me?
Duk. I remember you Sir, by the sound of your voice,
      I met you at the Prison, in the absence of the Duke

Luc. Oh, did you so? and do you remember what you said of the Duke

Duk. Most notedly Sir

Luc. Do you so Sir: And was the Duke a flesh-monger, a foole, and a coward, as you then reported him to be?

Duk. You must (Sir) change persons with me, ere you make that my report:
you indeede spoke so of him, and much more, much worse

Luc. Oh thou damnable fellow: did I not plucke thee by the nose, for thy
speeches?
Duk. I protest, I loue the Duke, as I loue my selfe

Ang. Harke how the villaine would close now, after his treasonable abuses

Esc. Such a fellow is not to be talk'd withall: Away with him to prison:
Where is the Prouost? away with him to prison: lay bolts enough
vpon him: let him speak no more: away with those Giglets too, and
with the other confederate companion

Duk. Stay Sir, stay a while

Ang. What, resists he? helpe him Lucio

Luc. Come sir, come sir, come sir: foh sir, why you bald-pated lying rascall:
you must be hooded must you? show your knaues visage with a poxe
to you: show your sheepe-biting face, and be hang'd an houre: Will't
not off?
Duk. Thou art the first knaue, that ere mad'st a Duke.
First Prouost, let me bayle these gentle three:
Sneake not away Sir, for the Fryer, and you,
Must haue a word anon: lay hold on him

Luc. This may proue worse then hanging

Duk. What you haue spoke, I pardon: sit you downe,
We'll borrow place of him; Sir, by your leaue:
Ha'st thou or word, or wit, or impudence,
That yet can doe thee office? If thou ha'st
Rely vpon it, till my tale be heard,
And hold no longer out

Ang. Oh, my dread Lord,

        I should be guiltier then my guiltinesse,
        To thinke I can be vndiscerneable,
        When I perceiue your grace, like powre diuine,
        Hath look'd vpon my passes. Then good Prince,
        No longer Session hold vpon my shame,
        But let my Triall, be mine owne Confession:
        Immediate sentence then, and sequent death,
        Is all the grace I beg

Duk. Come hither Mariana,
Say: was't thou ere contracted to this woman?
Ang. I was my Lord

Duk. Goe take her hence, and marry her instantly.
        Doe you the office (Fryer) which consummate,
        Returne him here againe: goe with him Prouost.

Enter.

Esc. My Lord, I am more amaz'd at his dishonor,
    Then at the strangenesse of it

Duk. Come hither Isabell,
        Your Frier is now your Prince: As I was then
        Aduertysing, and holy to your businesse,
        (Not changing heart with habit) I am still,
        Atturnied at your seruice

Isab. Oh giue me pardon
        That I, your vassaile, haue imploid, and pain'd
        Your vnknowne Soueraigntie

Duk. You are pardon'd Isabell:
        And now, deere Maide, be you as free to vs.
        Your Brothers death I know sits at your heart:
        And you may maruaile, why I obscur'd my selfe,
        Labouring to saue his life: and would not rather

       Make rash remonstrance of my hidden powre,
       Then let him so be lost: oh most kinde Maid,
       It was the swift celeritie of his death,
       Which I did thinke, with slower foot came on,
       That brain'd my purpose: but peace be with him,
       That life is better life past fearing death,
       Then that which liues to feare: make it your comfort,
       So happy is your Brother.

Enter Angelo, Maria, Peter, Prouost.

Isab. I doe my Lord

Duk. For this new-maried man, approaching here,
       Whose salt imagination yet hath wrong'd
       Your well defended honor: you must pardon
       For Mariana's sake: But as he adiudg'd your Brother,
       Being criminall, in double violation
       Of sacred Chastitie, and of promise-breach,
       Thereon dependant for your Brothers life,
       The very mercy of the Law cries out
       Most audible, euen from his proper tongue.
       An Angelo for Claudio, death for death:
       Haste still paies haste, and leasure, answers leasure;
       Like doth quit like, and Measure still for Measure:
       Then Angelo, thy fault's thus manifested;
       Which though thou would'st deny, denies thee vantage.
       We doe condemne thee to the very Blocke
       Where Claudio stoop'd to death, and with like haste.
       Away with him

Mar. Oh my most gracious Lord,
       I hope you will not mocke me with a husband?
       Duk. It is your husband mock't you with a husband,
       Consenting to the safe-guard of your honor,
       I thought your marriage fit: else Imputation,
       For that he knew you, might reproach your life,

And choake your good to come: For his Possessions,
Although by confutation they are ours;
We doe en-state, and widow you with all,
To buy you a better husband

Mar. Oh my deere Lord,
I craue no other, nor no better man

Duke. Neuer craue him, we are definitiue

Mar. Gentle my Liege

Duke. You doe but loose your labour.
Away with him to death: Now Sir, to you

Mar. Oh my good Lord, sweet Isabell, take my part,
Lend me your knees, and all my life to come,
I'll lend you all my life to doe you seruice

Duke. Against all sence you doe importune her,
Should she kneele downe, in mercie of this fact,
Her Brothers ghost, his paued bed would breake,
And take her hence in horror

Mar. Isabell:
Sweet Isabel, doe yet but kneele by me,
Hold vp your hands, say nothing: I'll speake all.
They say best men are moulded out of faults,
And for the most, become much more the better
For being a little bad: So may my husband.
Oh Isabel: will you not lend a knee?
Duke. He dies for Claudio's death

Isab. Most bounteous Sir.
Looke if it please you, on this man condemn'd,
As if my Brother liu'd: I partly thinke,
A due sinceritie gouerned his deedes,

Till he did looke on me: Since it is so,
Let him not die: my Brother had but Iustice,
In that he did the thing for which he dide.
For Angelo, his Act did not ore-take his bad intent,
And must be buried but as an intent
That perish'd by the way: thoughts are no subiects
Intents, but meerely thoughts

Mar. Meerely my Lord

Duk. Your suite's vnprofitable: stand vp I say:
    I haue bethought me of another fault.
    Prouost, how came it Claudio was beheaded
    At an vnusuall howre?
Pro. It was commanded so

Duke. Had you a speciall warrant for the deed?
Pro. No my good Lord: it was by priuate message

Duk. For which I doe discharge you of your office,
    Giue vp your keyes

Pro. Pardon me, noble Lord,
    I thought it was a fault, but knew it not,
    Yet did repent me after more aduice,
    For testimony whereof, one in the prison
    That should by priuate order else haue dide,
    I haue reseru'd aliue

Duk. What's he?
Pro. His name is Barnardine

Duke. I would thou hadst done so by Claudio:
    Goe fetch him hither, let me looke vpon him

Esc. I am sorry, one so learned, and so wise
    As you, Lord Angelo, haue stil appear'd,

>   Should slip so grosselie, both in the heat of bloud
>   And lacke of temper'd iudgement afterward
>
> Ang. I am sorrie, that such sorrow I procure,
>   And so deepe sticks it in my penitent heart,
>   That I craue death more willingly then mercy,
>   'Tis my deseruing, and I doe entreat it.

Enter Barnardine and Prouost, Claudio, Iulietta.

> Duke. Which is that Barnardine?
> Pro. This my Lord
>
> Duke. There was a Friar told me of this man.
>   Sirha, thou art said to haue a stubborne soule
>   That apprehends no further then this world,
>   And squar'st thy life according: Thou'rt condemn'd,
>   But for those earthly faults, I quit them all,
>   And pray thee take this mercie to prouide
>   For better times to come: Frier aduise him,
>   I leaue him to your hand. What muffeld fellow's that?
> Pro. This is another prisoner that I sau'd,
>   Who should haue di'd when Claudio lost his head,
>   As like almost to Claudio, as himselfe
>
> Duke. If he be like your brother, for his sake
>   Is he pardon'd, and for your louelie sake
>   Giue me your hand, and say you will be mine,
>   He is my brother too: But fitter time for that:
>   By this Lord Angelo perceiues he's safe,
>   Methinkes I see a quickning in his eye:
>   Well Angelo, your euill quits you well.
>   Looke that you loue your wife: her worth, worth yours
>   I finde an apt remission in my selfe:
>   And yet heere's one in place I cannot pardon,
>   You sirha, that knew me for a foole, a Coward,
>   One all of Luxurie, an asse, a mad man:

       Wherein haue I so deseru'd of you
       That you extoll me thus?
Luc. 'Faith my Lord, I spoke it but according to the trick: if you will hang me for it you may: but I had rather it would please you, I might be whipt

Duke. Whipt first, sir, and hang'd after.
       Proclaime it Prouost round about the Citie,
       If any woman wrong'd by this lewd fellow
       (As I haue heard him sweare himselfe there's one
       whom he begot with childe) let her appeare,
       And he shall marry her: the nuptiall finish'd,
       Let him be whipt and hang'd

Luc. I beseech your Highnesse doe not marry me to a Whore: your Highnesse said euen now I made you a Duke, good my Lord do not recompence me, in making me a Cuckold

Duke. Vpon mine honor thou shalt marrie her.
       Thy slanders I forgiue, and therewithall
       Remit thy other forfeits: take him to prison,
       And see our pleasure herein executed

Luc. Marrying a punke my Lord, is pressing to death,
       Whipping and hanging

Duke. Slandering a Prince deserues it.
       She Claudio that you wrong'd, looke you restore.
       Ioy to you Mariana, loue her Angelo:
       I haue confes'd her, and I know her vertue.
       Thanks good friend, Escalus, for thy much goodnesse,
       There's more behinde that is more gratulate.
       Thanks Prouost for thy care, and secrecie,
       We shall imploy thee in a worthier place.
       Forgiue him Angelo, that brought you home
       The head of Ragozine for Claudio's,
       Th' offence pardons it selfe. Deere Isabell,

I haue a motion much imports your good,
Whereto if you'll a willing eare incline;
What's mine is yours, and what is yours is mine.
So bring vs to our Pallace, where wee'll show
What's yet behinde, that meete you all should know.

The Scene Vienna.

THE NAMES OF ALL THE ACTORS

Vincentio: the Duke.
Angelo, the Deputie.
Escalus, an ancient Lord.
Claudio, a yong Gentleman.
Lucio, a fantastique.
2. Other like Gentlemen.
Prouost.
Thomas. 2. Friers.
Peter.
Elbow, a simple Constable.
Froth, a foolish Gentleman.
Clowne.
Abhorson, an Executioner.
Barnardine, a dissolute prisoner.
Isabella, sister to Claudio.
Mariana, betrothed to Angelo.
Iuliet, beloued of Claudio.
Francisca, a Nun.
Mistris Ouer-don, a Bawd.

FINIS.

Printed in the United States
143642LV00001B/2/P